Spiritual Journaling

God's Whispers in Daily Living

Spiritual Journaling

God's Whispers in Daily Living

Dan Kenneth Phillips

BOOKS

Winchester, UK
Washington, USA

First published by O-Books, 2011
O-Books is an imprint of John Hunt Publishing Ltd., Laurel House, Station Approach,
Alresford, Hants, SO24 9JH, UK
office1@o-books.net
www.o-books.com

For distributor details and how to order please visit the 'Ordering' section on our website.

Text copyright: Dan Kenneth Phillips 2010

ISBN: 978 1 84694 704 9

A CIP catalogue record for this book is available from the British Library.

Design: Lee Nash

Printed in the UK by CPI Antony Rowe
Printed in the USA by Offset Paperback Mfrs, Inc

We operate a distinctive and ethical publishing philosophy in all
areas of our business, from our global network of authors to
production and worldwide distribution.

CONTENTS

For Janet
My wonderful wife and encourager,
My companion on the journey.

Foreword

I have admired Dan Phillips and his spiritual writings for many, many years. He has a delightful and unique way of putting heartfelt experiences into the written word, "We have been crippled by time, leaks have appeared in our souls, we have hidden beneath the shadows ..." His journaling captures the spiritual essence of one's soul. Dan has a quiet disposition but a voracious thirst for spiritual knowledge and expression. He seeks to know the very heart of God. His first thought every morning is, "Lord, what do you have for me today? How am I going to see your hand at work in my life and the life of those you place in my path?"

Dan Phillips is a modern Renaissance Man. He is minister, webmaster, and pastor. He is a counselor, chaplain, and prayer leader. He is a preacher, teacher, traveler and retreat director. He is a life coach, a writer and journalist.

He is my spiritual mentor and true friend. A friend who has taught me how to begin, maintain and develop a lifelong Spiritual Journal. He has taught me how to look and listen for the Godly events; then, how to keep and savor them as reminders of an ever faithful God. The Israelites of ancient days would identify and mark their 'Godly events' by building alters or piling stones in order to mark and remember their spiritual happenings. Well, Brother Dan can teach you also, how to forever bring to remembrance these heartfelt experiences, which can be saved and continually drawn upon for encouragement and inspiration.

Dan Phillips has always had a unique ability to recognize and capture spiritual encounters. He picked up his journaling pen at 9 years old and never laid it down. In his book he shares his years of Spiritual experiences and teaches us what he has learned and how we can initiate and develop a Spiritual Journal of our own. He tells how we can listen for the very 'voice of God' in the quiet places of our lives and the lives of people we meet. Then, how to take these spiritual experiences and convert them into the written word and build these words, page upon page into our very own spiritual history journal. Dan tells us how to start, even what type of journal to purchase. He instructs us as to what to look and listen for and how to record these events into our written document. His insight teaches us that the most profound experience may me the smallest of experiences. Dan shows us how to look and listen for giant explosions of quiet revelation. The observation, recording and reviewing of these profound experiences can actually change our lives and the lives of friends and loved ones. The sharing of these recorded experiences will touch the hearts of all who listen.

There is so much that goes unnoticed in our hurried lives. The author teaches us how to seek out and nurture the experience of these miraculous moments which otherwise, may have gone undetected. He then clearly instructs us on how to translate these observations into written words in our journal, and relive them, time and time again. He talks of the importance of remembering the times of Gods' presence in our lives, then drawing on these spiritual encounters for encouragement in time of need.

Dan tells us how the words we write, "these words seasoned with salt," can be savored and cherished forever. They can bring remembrance, remembrance of a place and time when we felt the very presence of God. A time we never want to forget, a time when we reached out to the God of the universe and He placed his hand in ours. Let Brother Dan change and enrich your life by learning how to write and keep a Spiritual Journal.

Rich Nicorvo
Senior Vice-President, The Work Institute
Brentwood, Tennessee

Preface

For many years I have desired to write a book about Spiritual Journaling. I have kept spiritual journals most of my life. I have taught many workshops on Journaling and developed a website almost 15 years ago titled, "How to Develop A Spiritual Journal." The encouragement from those students in workshops, those midnight emails from discoverers of the journal site, and an editor who encouraged me have all been factors in developing this project.

My earliest remembrance of the importance of keeping words on paper goes back to the fourth grade at Smithwood Elementary School in Fountain City, Tennessee. My teacher was Mrs. Parkey. She explained the first week of school that she wanted each of us to keep a notebook dedicated to the quotes she wrote on the wall each day. Each morning she would come into the room, and without saying a word, write a quote on the blackboard.

I have kept those quotes through the years, thought I have temporarily misplaced them. Her favorite person to quote was B.C. Forbes and possibly Benjamin Franklin.

Several years later, I discovered a new employee I worked with who had gone to the same grammar school. When I ask him who had the greatest influence on him he said, "Mrs. Parkey." I thought, "what a great gift she had given us, the gift of the meaning of words."It is that gift I wish to share with you.

There are many people to thank on the journey, those who have been friends and encouraged me, colleagues, former students, conference personnel, and many others who have touched my life. These include:

Dear parents, Denman and Vallie Phillips, who loved and encouraged me, Janet Phillips, my dear wife, who stood by my side, Melinda, our daughter, always one who makes us proud, Mike, her husband, who keeps my computer running, and Jack, our grandson, who is always trying to figure out what Poppa is doing, and Ronald, my brother, who always remembers the important things.

And especially, Richard Nicorvo, who kept encouraging me to write a book, Wayne Burns, who often went on some of my spiritual adventures, George Clark, humorist and joyful companion, who often used what God was doing in our lives as fodder for his own writings, Joe Johnson, editor par-excellent who kept me writing for over three decades, and The Rock Group, The Saturday Night Bunch, The Developing Your Spiritual Life Sunday School Class, and Gary, Laura, Carlos, Pamela, Larry, Joe, Lynn, and many, many others, and especially my publisher and editor, Timothy Staveteig, for his encouragement and ability to say the right word at the right time.

We do not go this journey alone. May this book be a reminder of the influence each of you had on my life.

Introduction

Beginning Thoughts

I am a member of the Christian community. Although a lifelong member of the Baptist church, I have been blessed by being able to lead retreats in Episcopal churches, Catholic retreat centers, non-denominational retreat centers, Baptist conference communities, Christian churches pastor's retreats, and in dozens of states to churches that allowed me to share inspirations in my life. I have been blessed by these brethren. They have instilled a respect and love for their struggles in the Christian faith. They have enlightened me, challenged me, and offered me gifts that have reflected our struggles together.

As I reflect on this, I hold in my hand a salmon paperweight given to me by a lady in British Columbia. The conference I led there was entirely without notes because all of the materials I had sent from Tennessee never arrived. The salmon is a reminder that, in spite of our weaknesses, God can still use us.

Spiritual Journaling, God's Whispers in Daily Living, is a book of my experiences keeping spiritual journals. Over four decades of journals sit in my study. Each has a message and reflects a time of God's work in my life. Some of the journals are difficult to bring myself to remember, because some of the days were dark and heavy. Other journals are filled with joy when I remember God's presence.

Ira Progoff's, At A Journal Workshop, is a pivotal book in my journey. I went to my first one in Monteagle, Tennessee, in August of 1980. It was shortly after my father had died. I was lost. I was alone. I was afraid. For three days we sat in a room silently and wrote. The meditative aspects of that silence and writing became for me a discipline of prayer and reflection, the focusing on the importance of journaling. The silence became the Stirring of the Wind, the still small voice spoken in absolute quietness.

When Ezra found the holy book in Jerusalem, he read it continuously for hours. It was not only a treasure but a journey of God's Holiness to his people. (Nehemiah 8:3)

In my first chapter, Whispers in the Wind, I explore the importance of silence on the journey. I follow Elijah's journey, across the slopes of Mount Carmel, where I find the point where God speaks through the Still Small Voice, a whisper, that is always the starting point for writing in a spiritual journal, the place where God speaks. It is a precious hour, an hour of remembrance that need not be forgotten. It is about tiny words slung across the universe. It is about Sacred Time, a quiet time of celebration of God's vision for us.

The second chapter describes the Buffalo Hunter's Journal, a story of the importance to me of the type of journal we use. It should be a book capable of capturing our lives while the battle is raging. It should reflect the tears, the victories, the bent pages that reflect the trials and the winning smiles mellowing our faces. It is about making the book worthy.

The Power of Words, the third chapter, shows the importance of every word we speak, the words of accountability, and how a lady dying of cancer named Bonnie showed the importance of the words we speak. It is an account of being there in the midst of strange sentences and seeing a spark of God's aliveness. It brings accountability to the pages that fill our journal. Even the silence between the words becomes important in this chapter.

The fourth chapter is about Mind the Gap, a phrase used in London every time a tube (subway) train stops. "Mind the Gap!" Be aware of the moment. It is a short time. The moment you will forget if you do not jump. I have heard that if you do not write it down, you will forget it. That is true. This chapter is about anointing each minute, writing quickly as God speaks to us. The date, and the location, become the framework of what God is doing in us.

A Passion for Place, the fifth chapter, is about those places we stop to get our lives in order or to discover that special something that God has been waiting to show us. These places of pilgrimage define who we are, those unexpected hours where God touches us. We need to record those moments in our journal, those places where Jesus walked on the water, or we heard His words clearly. These pilgrimages are about our searching for a meaning in a world clamored with fake itineraries that are suppose to make us happy.

Chapter six is about Praying. When we pray it again brings me to those places where God has been valid. Our prayers become the window of our spiritual life. They are the most important hours. They need reflection, whether it is being lost in a busy city and we cry out for direction, or a wandering stranger with drenched pages of his prayer journal in his pocket.

The Unexpected Guest, chapter seven, may remind me of Nathanial Hawthorne's stories, but it tells of stories in my own life that I have written down of Unexpected Guests in my life. It is so easy to miss them because most are hidden, strangers unaware, maybe unexpected bumps in the road. But we do not forget. They are the Elisha's that Elijah had to find after the Still Small Voice, the ones crying in the wilderness. These guests are highlighted in my spiritual journal. They are visionary, sometimes with just one message for us, a message to change our lives. They are the Timothy events, the times of challenge, and stories worth remembering.

Storms, chapter eight, is about stormy weather, those periods when dark shadows dim our vision, when we are frail and without strength, moments when we question our motivations, times we decide and are undecided. We become afraid of facing tomorrow. We are scared. These treasures in the darkness, written in our journal when we were ambiguous about life, become the later meaning of our lives. The messes become messages of God's use for us.

Days of Recollection, chapter nine, take moments of our lives in a retreat setting to reflect and seek God in our life.

Fragments, chapter ten, takes the leftovers of our life and discovers uses for them. These are the fish and loaves of our lives, the tiny steps across the road that make a difference in other's lives. This is about the importance of the unexpected, the making beauty out of ugliness, the holding on when the boat is about to sink. It is using the left hand after the right hand has been taken from us. It is the the two fish that become miracles and everyone stands in amazement at the result. Yes, it is the fragments in our lives that become the miracles.

Magical Journeys, chapter eleven, closes the book. A spiritual journal is a magical journey. It is the story of our life, written by us, to give back to others. A friend of mine, who runs a fountain pen shop, told me recently that since 9/11 she has sold more journals than ever in her life. "People want something left of their lives to share with others," she said. After 9/11 there were a lot of blank pages for thousands of persons. We are each on a magical journey and every page is a discovery when we re-read our spiritual journals.

Thoughts

What have I learned in my decades of journal writing? I have learned that each moment can be a revelation, that the amount or number of words used is not nearly as important as the message, and honoring our spiritual journals means we have focused on those moments when God speaks to us and they are worth remembering.

This book is a focused on the spiritual moments in my life. points of remembrance, the still small voice, the whisper in the wind, the hidden word, the points of light like a meteor showering the sky.

I hope you will use this book as a beginning point for your own spiritual journey. This is not so much a how to do book as what are the important things in our life worth remembering.

Start by buying that special journal, maybe one that is expensive, and write notes to yourself as you read, as you experience life, as you go about living. Write. Write. Write! Add notes and reflections and about the flowers you have seen blooming. And if, if you get stuck just remember:

Pause!
Silence!
Write!

I

Whispers in the Wind

"Deep within us all there is an amazing inner sanctuary of the soul, a holy place, a Divine Center, a speaking voice, to which we may continuously return." (Thomas Kelly)

My journal always goes with me. The most used is the 3.5x5.5 inch Moleskine pocket journal. It easily fits in my back pocket, or my inside coat pocket. Before I go to work I make sure it is with me. When I went to various countries in Europe this was the journal I carried. It has enough pages for useful information, thoughts, and notes on the historical character of the cities I visit. The portability is important! It can be used anywhere, a subway station, bus, train, airplane, a coffee shop table, standing up, or sitting down, anywhere.

I like having a journal with me. I feel it is an easy companion. It doesn't complain, seems happy when I write in it, is not accusing, easily closes, gets out of the way when I need it to sleep, and is always silent. The words placed in it are usually a secret, or a vision, or a hope or dream. It can also be a place of contradictions, of complaints, of lists that need to be considered,

The journey with a journal is like an awakening. It is an hour of anticipation. A sacred time. A mystery takes place as one begins to write. The presence of the moment, enhanced from the readings from the Bible, become real. Prayer becomes a friend. The journal, like a prayer partner, listens to the words as they are written down in thinly streaked lines, softly written, an heir of sacred illumination. Time becomes distorted, the word, present and active, brings a stillness, an hour of solitude.

For over twenty years I have taken Anne Morrow Lindberg's

A Gift from the Sea on my trips to the beach. She talks about beach time, the moment when one is not influenced by the to do list, but by the rhythms of the ocean. Like a new vision of the world, a journal can be like that, a place to place the lessons of life, the fears of the moment, a presenting of the life we have and are. Like bread offered during the Lord's Supper, it is a remembrance, an offering to God, the words, spoken or unspoken, written or unwritten, thoughts begun or ended. There is a grace about the hour. A grace delivering forgiveness and hope.

Blessing

On a morning between the chill of winter and the heat of summer, I sit on my patio, listen to a symphony of birds, sit in my adirondack chair, and place my hands over the turned pages of the journal. It is like a blessedness, a blessing for the hours. At the hospital, where I am chaplain, many times I have been requested to bless an office where someone is moving to for the first time. I usually go alone, no strangers are needed, and go from room to room, or office to office, saying a blessing to remove the dangerous spirits of life and fill the rooms with love

I once heard the story of Dr. James Sullivan, president of the Baptist Sunday School Board, who was an early riser, often getting to work before 5 a.m. The story was told that often he would go to different offices throughout the building, sit in the chair of the occupant, and say a prayer for them. A journal is like that, an instrument of sacredness and blessing. "May you bless my words," I say, as I begin.

"In Rivendell all of them grew refreshed and strong. Their clothes were mended as well as their bruises, their tempers, and their hopes. Their bags were filled with food and provisions light to carry but strong to bring them over the mountain passes. Their plans were improved with the best advice. Now they rode away amid songs of farewell and good speed, with their hearts ready for more adventure, and with a knowledge of the road they must follow over Misty Mountains to the Land Beyond," wrote J.R.R. Tolkien in the Hobbit.

It sounds like a journal moment of blessedness, the hour of new beginnings, new thoughts that enlighten the day. My prayer is often one of saying simply, "Lord, use me today, to do thy will." It is often enough.

Silence

My first step before any journal entry is a time of silence. It may be for a minute, five minutes, or longer. It is the time when the phone is off the hook, the newspaper is closed, the cup of coffee has been reheated, the house has been emptied, and the spot I have chosen, my cave, is filled with silence.

In those moments I expect nothing. I may hear the wind, the storm passing, an ambulance screaming near the hospital behind my house, or a dog barking in the distance. None of this really matters. This is always the starting point, waiting for the still small voice, the whisper, maybe the muse, to begin. It is a sacred moment. Waiting! Waiting. Sometimes I fold my hands and open my spiritual journal to the page where I will begin writing.

In 2009, I traveled with several others to Israel. One of our stops was atop Mount Carmel. Mount Carmel is 1,810 feet high, covers approximately 4-5 miles, and oversees the Valley of Jezreel. The view is spectacular. For hundreds of miles one can watch for enemies' arrivals, or in Elijah's case, look for a cloud indicating rain after years of drought.

On the mountain we celebrated Elijah's victory over the 450 prophet's of Baal. We gathered in a circle, read scripture from 1 Kings 18, held hands, and prayed. When the others headed toward the bus, I hustled inside the the Stella Maris monastery next door and prayed in the chapel.

According to tradition, the altar covers the cave where Elijah once shared all his troubles with God. "Lord, I am the only one left." (1 Kings 10:10) It was a time of discouragement. Ahab's wife, Jezebel, had placed a death sentence on him, seeking his immediate death. "Elijah was afraid and ran for his life," says 1 Kings 19:3. According to my calculations he ran for over 70 miles. On the journey he prayed that he might die. "I have had enough, Lord. Take my life." (1 Kings 19:4)

Certainly, we have all had those moments that impossible odds seem to face us; the death of a loved one, the loss of a job, a faithful friend angry at us, someone accusing us unjustly, a wavering moment of fear, and maybe destruction of once highlighted dreams.

It is during that devastating period in his life that God begins to speak to Elijah, "Go out and stand on the mountain in the presence of the Lord, for the Lord is about to pass by." Afterwards there are powerful winds tearing the mountain apart, there was an earthquake, then a fiery mountain of flames, but each time there was the shattered refrain, "the Lord did not speak through these catastrophic events." How often we struggle to hear the voice during the storms of life, only to find them drowned out by comfortless messages further focusing on our deteriorating condition.

But then, there was the *"still small voice,"* a gentle whisper. When Elijah heard the voice he covered his head with his cloak and moved to the mouth of the cave to hear more.

Listening

The Abbey of Gethsemani, a trappist monastery in Trappist, Kentucky, near Bardstown, Kentucky, is near. In 1848 the foundation began. It has lingered as a spiritual pilgrimage spot for over 150 years. On the table, where one eats, is always a sign, "Silence is spoken here." As I eat the simple fare of a trappist monastery, the sign is the reminder, I am a gladiator of stillness and this is the beginning point for great adventures with God, the Silence, the wordlessness of the hour, the waiting for the whisper in the wind.

As dusk turns off the light of day, one enters The Great Silence, a time of complete quiet. I remember my first night in the great silence. The rains had stopped and our retreat leader said, "Tonight when we conclude our evening prayers, you are not to speak to anyone, including your mate, until we finish our first meal in the morning. We will be entering *The Great Silence.*

"What is this *"Great Silence,"* I wondered. But, I will always remember that night. I limped in darkness with only a small beam of light as a guide. With every step were the noises of night, a wayward bird, the howl of a distant dog, an airplane above carrying passengers to the other side of the continent, and cars passing in darkness and blowing their horns. Although it was not fearful, it was an awakening. Sounds were magnified. Listening became paramount.

I will never forget the next morning. The silence continued as we began eating our breakfast. I remember the clicking of the forks and spoons, and particularly the crash of my hard-boiled egg against others plates. It was both embarrassing and revealing. Without voices stirring one began to listen for God. Something unexplainable was happening in our lives.

When we could talk again, our words were different. No frivolous words entered our conversations. Every word had meaning. Laughter was limited. It was if our language had been transformed so that we used the minimum number of words possible for communication. And surprisingly, we discovered that true communication did not always require words.

During a recent visit to the Abbey, Father Anton, the guest master said, *"When the bells ring, it is the voice of God calling us to prayer."* And he continued, *"Listening for God's Voice is why we are here."*

Listening is difficult for those of us whose lives are modulated by screaming televisions with commercials programmed 10 decibels above the regular programming, honking cars precariously pass by our meditation points, loud chatter occurs in an adjoining room, and fitful imaginings fill our minds.

So silence, listening for the still small voice, a gentle whisper, becomes our motto for beginning a spiritual journal. The Great Silence is the beginning step for a spiritual journey that changes our lives.

The whisper in the wind I call it. A moment of blessing. The silence. The listening... The moment when each sacred journey of writing begins. The listening for the wind to speak.!

2

The Buffalo Hunter Journal

"Our stories are written beneath the lines in the journal, often broken words that linger." (The Author)

On Buying a Spiritual Journal

I keep an old baseball that Stan Musial once hit. I was a teenager, the Cardinals were playing the Cubs in an exhibition game in Knoxville, Tennessee. Mr. Rosenbaum, a former minor leaguer, knew of my love for baseball, so he took me to the game because one of his friends played for the Cubs.

Somehow I ended up with a baseball Stan Musial hit that day. I took it home and cared for it, but as time passed, there were days we lost the baseball we were playing with, and so we sometimes threw the Musial ball back and forth. Then tempted, we hit the ball with the bat. Now, the ball is worn. It is frayed! A shell of what it was, but still, in spite of no name on it, it is the *Stan Musial Baseball*, an heirloom of a past era but sacred in its meaning to my life.

A frayed journal is precious like that baseball. It often has torn pages, water lines dribbled throughout, ink stains scattered, forgotten names in inappropriate places, words misspelled, tear stains shed on blotted ink, raindrops from hurried trips in the rain, ripped pages of anger, marked through forgotten names, crayon marks of a child, bible verses faintly scribbled in darkness, articles from deceased newspaper columnists, sports headlines of victories and defeats, wrinkled pages, a running commentary on daily events, names of deceased friends and their obituaries, a running commentary of our spiritual journey.

Buffalo Hunter Journal

In Red Lodge, Montana, while doing a retreat for 25 pastors on spirituality, I became intrigued by a journal I found at the Red Lodge Bookstore. I did not buy it the first time I saw it, but returned after the retreat was over to buy it as a way of remembering the importance of those days in my life. The journal would reflect those moments. It was a Buffalo Hunter's Journal, 5" x 7", just the right size for placing my torn covered NIV Bible inside.

The Advertisement

"This 'Oh-sooo-soft' leather is double thick with a natural tattered rough edge. the kind a traveler may have taken with them on that long journey, chasing the western sunset. Coptic bound, so it always lays open flat. Each is one of a kind."

I admit I have certain obsessions; unique leather bound journals, fountain pens, combs, pocket knives, and coin purses. Things that can be easily lost traveling. I bought the Buffalo Hunter's Journal and stuffed it in the bag to carry back on the airplane. It has become, like many of my journals, special reminders of special times of spiritual discover, they shadow me wherever I go. The notes in them are reminders of the journey.

In the buffalo journal I wrote; "It was snowing when I arrived in Red Lodge, Montana. The temperature was 19 degrees the next morning. I slept in a cabin by Rock Creek. There were no indoor facilities. Deer roamed freely outside the cabin. I shared my vision of God with 25 pastors while there. We ate together, shared the extreme difficulties of being a pastor in a place with few people, and delighted in each other's stories. The buffalo journal reflects the courage of a time I was called to listen and speak of what I heard in the desert landscape filled with snow".

When I write in the Buffalo Hunter Journal, I feel the Montana cold, see the eyes of the pastors as they listened to me speak, remember that while there I had a devilish arthritic knee and every step was agony, and I can still remember the brightness of the stars and the silence surrounding the stilled darkness.

A journal is an important reminder of a time and place when we were alive and remembering the face of the days surrounding us. A journal should have a feel of importance about it. In earlier days I wasn't as sensitive to the type of journal used. I often used cheap 5x8 notebooks picked up at a drug store. I could fill one in a month, trying mostly to put down anything that came into my mind.

As time went on, I begin to feel that these notes were important and needed to be respected, at least in a journal that would last and one I could be proud of as I carried it around as a friend. My favorite journals are the Moleskine journals designed by an Italian company.

These journals have character about them. Included with each of them is a history lesson on the journal:

"Moleskine is the legendary notebook, used by European artists and thinkers for the past two centuries, from Van Gogh to Picasso, from Ernest Hemingway to Bruce Chatwin. This trusty, pocket-size travel companion held sketches, notes, stories and ideas before they were turned into famous images or pages of beloved book." The story continues that the Moleskine is used *"to capture reality on the move, pin down details, impress upon paper unique aspects of experience: Moleskine is a reservoir of ideas and feelings, a battery that stores discoveries and perceptions, and who energy can be tapped over time."*

My favorite part is that it is a battery that stores discoveries and perceptions. What an enticement! Every word counts. Writing in it is a tradition that follows the footprints of some of the most influential persons throughout history.

These journals are available in most large book stores. The pages are made of a special acid-free paper that "feels" good to write on. There is a quality about the pages. I usually use a fountain pen when writing in a 5x8.5 inch Moleskine journal I use. I feel that the ink of fountain pens helps my creativity. The ink flowing has a feel of emotion, it quiets my spirit, and helps me in exploring the thoughts I am seeking to arrange. Writing on a page can be uneven. I can write sideways, or just scribble quickly in the margins, sometimes even writing left-handed to increase the creative spark.

In spite of carefully protecting them, because I often carry them with me, I still wear them out. I drop them in the rain or spill ink on portions of them. But, within their pages, are inspirational words that often become an excavation point in my life.

I once had a seminary professor who would bring eight or nine books to each class he taught. He emphasized that he knew we would not read the books, but that we could at least say that we had seen them. He also had a habit of smelling of each book, telling us each book had a smell that was directly related to that book and that, before reading any book, he would smell it first. Now, at the time I thought that was crazy, but the more I consider it, the more it makes sense. With a journal, sniffing is a way of identification, a way of personalizing the writing that will, or has been written. A way of blessing the importance of the words placed.

Sporadic quotes, or scriptural insights, are like seeds planted in the journal. They often bear fruit later. As the seeds are planted, the journal gathers strength in helping us with out daily excursions. It becomes more powerful as it is used and more important in our lives. As the years pass re-reading brings remembrances of God's presence in our lives. The permanence of a journal that will last is a prized possession.

The importance of a spiritual journal is that it gathers strength in helping us with our daily excursions through our days. This type of journal has a feel of permanence and it will last.

A Spiritual Journal Master

I once went on a retreat to Penuel Ridge Retreat Center in Ashland City, Tennessee. There were several spiritual books on the shelves. One was "The Private Devotions of Lancelot Andrewes." I found myself writing quotes from this book in my journal, filling up several pages. Each time I returned, I copied more pages. I fruitlessly tried to find a copy at local bookstores in the mid- 80s. In August of 1999, I was able to get a full copy of this book from Peter Smith Publishers. The book is important to me for several reasons; the character of Andrewes, his powerful use of words and scripture, and the size of the book.

Andrewes was one of the original members of the committee that translated the King James Version of the Bible. The Reverend John Buckeridge, in Andrewes funeral sermon, said, "His life was a life of prayer. A great part of five hours every day did he spend in prayer to God. His prayer book, when he was in private, was seldom seen out of his hands. The Private Devotions is a monument of these hours of devotion, in which he first tested for himself what he has bequeathed for us."

I am especially impressed with his use of scripture to convey meanings beyond my original thoughts. Scripture becomes prayer in his hands. William Law, to whom Andrewes gave his journals, described best what was the probably the method of Andrewes, said, "If people were to collect the best forms of devotion, to use themselves to transcribe the finest passages of Scripture-prayer; if they were to collect the devotions, confessions, petitions, praises, resignations and thanksgivings which are scattered up and down in the Psalms and range them under proper heads as so much proper fuel for the flame of their own devotion; if their minds were often thus employed, sometimes meditating upon them, sometimes getting them by heart and making them as habitual as their own thoughts, how fervently would they pray, who came thus prepared to pray."

For several years of reading the Private Devotions I have often

20

wondered, "how many journals did he have to fill in order to write this book?" Several I thought. Recently, while doing further research I discovered that the book that he used was a given to his friend William Laud, who wrote on the front cover, "My Reverend Friend Bishop Andrewes gave me this book a little before his death." The book is 188 pages, 168 of them filled, and is 5 inches by 2-1/2 inches. I was astonished when I read that because the journal I was using at the time was 192 pages, 5-1/4 inches by 3-1/2. I had carried this journal from April 15, 2009, until February 11, 2011. I was surprised that the words I wrote roughly approached the same length as the Private Devotions. That was an important moment for me. It was a realization that every word we placed in a journal could influence others.

A page in this journal is still memorable to me. It was written after midnight on a cold starry night on a retreat at Camp Hillmont in Tennessee. It is my paraphrase of the 23rd Psalm:

Psalm 23
The Lord cares for me
I have need for nothing
He gives me a night of quiet rest
He feeds me with the silence of His Word
My life has new hope
His guidance leads me through the darkness.

He is with me
Through the dark night of the soul
His touch ever with me
His hand quietly on my shoulder

When the enemy comes
He is there
With oil
With grace

With his presence and mercy
And I will ever be His.

Sometimes I write scripture on the pages, much like Andrewes, but most of the time it involves words, or shall I call it, silences between the words, that are meaningful to me.

If a small pocket journal can be a discovery of spiritual development in our lives, it is worth working on. Yes, our lives are frayed like the Buffalo Hunter Journal. We have been crippled by time, leaks have appeared in our souls, we have hidden beneath the shadows, climbed tedious mountains, danced while in sorrow, sat alone under weighed branches, been deceived, trespassed against our neighbor, lusted after that which is not ours, been afraid of the darkness, and wandered alone in isolated shadows. Such is the life that has chosen us, or that we have chosen.

Our path has often been unpure. There are discrepancies in our lives. Our journals pilgrimage our choices and show light that has broadened our path.

Writing about the closed doors, hurtful actions, sunrises that are memorable, and the disguises I often wear can be placed as stories in the journal that beckon us back to the spiritual meanings of the moment. Our stories are written beneath the lines in the journal, often broken words that linger. The words between the lines have captured my life. Scripture verses have motivated me. Our journals are often filled with choices. Do we write, or not? Why place words on a page, can't I just remember them? You know the answer to that. Get that expensive journal you pass by and use it as a reflection of God's work in your life.

3

The Power of Words

"Write only in your journal when something grips you or has special meaning to you."

One of the biggest questions I get related to journal writing is how often should I write in the journal. My answer always seems to surprise them. Only write when something grips you or has a special meaning. Do not waste words because they are powerful and important.But do write when the words touch you.

In writing in my journal, I often scatter sentences in different directions on the page. The words may be sideways, upside down, or even a sentence the length of a page written in large letters. The direction on the page may say more about what I am trying to convey than the neatness. I may draw an uneven picture. In one journal is a picture drawn while sitting in a chair beneath a mountain in North Carolina. It was a time of high spiritual significance to me during a time of great loss. The Adirondack chair I sat in was as much a part of the message as the picture. Often my words are scattered in a less than a dignified format on a page. That is part of the inspiration, the way they fit in the spiritual journal.

Words are strange. By themselves they can lead nowhere, but stack them together and rumbling dynamics of meaning rush off the page with renewed energy. Every page can be a discovery as we reread our journals. The number of words used is not nearly as important as the message they convey. They give depth to a day and often add important knowledge to an experience. They often surprise, or make us sad. They can uplift us joyously, or bring us to tears. But a journal without words is not a journal.

In a spiritual journal the words are placed in a framework of God's presence. They are not written except they have an unlisted meaning, sometimes precariously hidden deep between sentences.

A Journey of Healing

As I write these words, I am preparing for a journey. Each week I teach courses on spirituality to hospital patients. After initial thoughts on spirituality, usually revolving around the 23rd Psalm and its messages of restoration and guidance, I share a story with them. It is about Bonnie. For over twenty years Bonnie worked in this hospital. She was vivacious, always a smile on her face, always late! She beamed all over when she talked of her travels with her husband, Jack, as they traveled around the world. Her most meaningful place was the Garden of Gethsemani in Jerusalem, beneath the Mount of Olives.

When she turned 50 she received bad news, she discovered she had a form of leukemia. Her attitude toward her disease was different than others. She did not whine, "why did this happen to me, I am a good person." Her refrain was, "this will give me a chance to meet others who are going through the same situation and I can share my faith with them." That was the path she followed. Always upbeat, ready to share about her new friends she met while taking chemotherapy.

Sometimes she would have to check into the hospital for a few days. She brought her favorite blanket, a stack of CD's to listen to, cards to write to her friends, and the funny little sailor's hat she wore because of her baldness due to treatments.

Her hospital room became a sanctuary. Everyone brought their problems to her because she was a person who would pray for them. And her favorite phrase was, "Brother Dan, let me tell you what God has done for me today." Her room was anointed with the possibilities of what each of us could become. It was room of spiritual depth, where GRACE stood beside her each

24

moment. When one of our nurses lost their mother and father in a car accident, it was Bonnie who called us all together and prayed for the nurse. That nurse's life was changed because of taking care of Bonnie. Many lives were changed because of her witness.

But there came a day when news was not good. She no longer responded to the treatment. Her days were numbered. She began planning what she wanted to do; one more trip to the beach and a weekend that she wanted to spent in retreat with her closest friends.

Before her final journey she came to me and said, "Brother Dan, I have a message I would like to share with my friends, and I need to do it now because I will not be able to much longer."

Bonnie's request was important. She had become a wonderful friend. I had seen her battle cancer with amazing strength, resilience, and an attitude that every moment she lived was important. She kept an elaborate spiritual journal with a special emphasis on the people who came into her life that day and brought blessings. She would often say to me when I visited her hospital room, "Brother Dan, these are the things God is doing in my life today."

We made arrangements quickly for her to speak. Her time was dimming and she only lived two more weeks, but when she spoke in chapel the room was full. People from all areas of the hospital showed up and she shared with us what she called, "The Power of Words." I copied the words she shared in my journal and often share with others as Bonnie's final sermon.

The Sermon

"The first thing we should realize is that we can be hurt by words. People may have given you an inappropriate nickname when you were small and you have hung it around your neck like a continuous revelation all of your life. Be careful of the words you say about another.

What words do you feed yourself? What do you say about yourself? Are you positive or is the continuous ring in your life a tedious journey downward. Look closely at what you say about yourself. Do you emphasize the positive things about your life or are you always looking at the negative?

Who influenced your life? What words did they use? Chances are that someone who influenced your life the most was someone who used words that were meaningful to you.. They emphasized your strengths and told you the things you were good at. They were always excited to see you and share in the new adventures in your life. All of us should be aware of the words we share with others. Maybe the words "seasoned with salt" will change some ones life for good."

She concluded that section of her message with a quote from Mother Theresa, "We leave people better than we found them." We need to be able to answer that question with a yes that we helped someone with their lives.

In her conclusion, Bonnie shared the four phrases that mean the most in our lives: "These really matter," she said. These are the Most Important Words You Will Ever Say:

1. "I love you! This is the most important phrase we will ever say," said Bonnie. As she said this I remembered a trip I made to my Uncle Herbert, whom I loved very much. He was about to die and I was about to get married. I asked him, "Uncle Herbert do you have any advice for someone about to get married." His answer was firm. "Always tell your wife I Love You every day of your life." I have faithfully followed those words for over four decades of marriage. Bonnie's words ring true.

2. "I'm sorry, please forgive me! She said, "Never be afraid to say I'm sorry!"

3. "I forgive you.! "These may be the most difficult words we ever say," she said.

4. Say Thank You!

She concluded by repeating, "These are the words that matter most in life." And then she said, "The righteous weight their words, and kind words can be short but their echoes are endless."

Words in a journal do not have to be profound, but there should be a stirring of the spirit that attends them. A word fitly spoken can make all of the difference. I often re-read Bonnie's words and when others hear her story I feel it makes a difference.

Everlasting Words

Frank Varallo Jr., a friend of mine, passed away recently. He was 93 years young. During the past few years he has been a patient at our hospital. He was also known for running Varallo's Restaurant which was located on Church Street in Nashville, Tennessee. It has a history of being the oldest restaurant in town.

I ate there often. I loved his famous 3-way lunch special, consisting of chili, a tamale, and spaghetti. It was a place of laughter and we were always greeted as if we were the only customers in the world. Vic Varallo, his nephew, manned the cash register and Frank and his wife Eva kept the food moving.

He and Eva celebrated their 70th wedding anniversary this weekend, one day before he died. On a recent wedding anniversary Eva wrote to Frank:

"I want to tell you again how much I love you and cherish each day we have shared both good and bad. I thank the Lord each day for having let our paths cross, our hearts meet and blossom into a deep and abiding love."

It's quotes like that I keep in my spiritual journal, minor words with dynamite meanings. They are words not easily forgotten. They are not only reminders of love, but of a caring for one person to another.

Remember what I said at the first of this chapter? What should I write in my journal? Write only in your journal when something grips you or has special meaning to you. "When words grab you," write them down. Listen for the right words, and when you hear them, place them in your journal, that's where the power of words changes your life.

4

Mind the Gap

"Please mind the gap between the train and the platform."

It took me several days to properly understand the London Subway (Tube) system. I entered every train with a step of trepidation. Where will this lead? What if I transfer at the wrong place? Is my map right? Am I pointed east or west, north or south? Before my first trip to London, England, in May of 2007, I had never heard the phrase Mind the Gap. With my first tube ride, I became aware that Mind the Gap over the loud speaker on the train was important. It was used as a precautionary notice to prevent passengers from suffering injury by stepping in the wide gap before train arrival at a station. A misstep could be fatal.

Be Aware of the Moment
"Write fast, write everything, include everything, write from your feelings, write from your body, accept whatever comes," were words written by Tristine Rainer in her classic work, The New Diary. Those words are a reminder that a careful footing of our lives makes our journey easier, safer, and more meaningful. For a spiritual journey, no words could be more appropriate.

Another way of calculating the journey is to be aware of the moment. Life is short. I have heard that if you do not write it down, you will forget it. That is so true. This chapter is about anointing each minute, writing quickly so not to fall from the grace that follows us, and reflecting on the greater flow of God in our lives.

The date, the location, the emotional experience of God's work in us becomes the frameworks of how God is working in our lives. It is so easy to forget, maybe the story, or the event, or how we got there. We surely did not start out in this direction. We were headed north, not south. But God spoke a second time and the journey began. There were common travelers on the trip. They may have been hidden in the darkness but it made a difference. Our spiritual journals should reflect those moments, those times when God spoke to us, those gap moments of awareness.

Date

Nothing is as important in a spiritual journal as the writing down of the date when we place an entry. That is the first thing I do. I write the date, the day of the week, the temperature, and often I title each day.

Taking my journal and looking at March 15, 2006, I spoke in chapel where I work and told of the influence of Jimmy Caldwell. His obituary said he was 106 years old when he died. It followed with, "he is survived by 22 grandchildren, several great grand-children, and great great grandchildren and great great great grandchildren." These were beginning words on our influence on others.

May 6, 2006, was a Day of Recollection. It was highlighted with a poem by a blogging friend, Anthony Hanson, called To "The Quiet."

I need time to make some decisions
Discernment
I need more than just a few days of retreat
I need some time in the desert
I need to remove as many distractions as possible
I need to "seek God."

Sometimes I fill my journal with just scripture and some thoughts. On a Sunday, November 13, 2005, with it raining and the temperature 59 degrees I wrote: "Hear, read, mark, learn, and inwardly digest – the scriptures." Then, I wrote the word embrace. Embrace means so much more in defining our relationship to the scriptures. On the same day my prayer of the heart was, "that I might be a light in the darkness." The day was closed by a quote from the monk Matthew Kelty: "We ain't perfect, but we tried, we did the best we could."

Dating an entry also provides a help in remembrance of when an events and their importance. happened. We can remember birthdates, anniversaries, and other important events. But each day, dated, leaves an impression that God spoke to us when we have recorded his word in our spiritual journals.

Location

It was London. It was raining. It was a Saturday. The date was May 12, 2007. London is a busy city. Most people use the tube, the subway, for transportation. On work days customers wear dress clothes and carry a backpack. Radio stations are virtually useless. I have yet to hear a weather report on one. Every day is the same, wet and windy, 55 degrees, and the sun will peak out of the clouds at least twice a day. Hale spirits are needed to buffet the daily weather. Lots of people smoke, especially the younger ladies, and when eating in pubs lots of laughter and noise accompany the smoke and ale. They are a reverend people, especially related to their heritage. They appreciate the history and understand the past much better than us.

My number one goal in going to London was to see Westminster Abbey. Officially it is The Collegiate Church of St Peter, Westminster. A million persons visit each year. An advertisement says it is "a living church, a royal peculiar, home to the unique pageant of British history. It is traditionally the place of coronation and burial site for leaders of the monarch."

At noon we had checked into the Crowne Plaza London St. James Hotel on Buckingham Gate. It had been a long night. We had spent sleepless hours on the airplane from Charlotte, North

Carolina. We checked into the hotel and took a nap. About 3:30 p.m., we awoke and decided to go to Westminster Abbey. On the map it seemed like a short distance, from 51 Buckingham Gate, southward to Victoria Street, and eastward to the Abbey.

We arrived at the Abbey at 4 p.m. The sign said the entrance fee was 15 pounds for adults, which was more than we expected. It also said that the last time for entrance was 3:30. A secondary note indicated that if we attended a worship service, we could view the Abbey without cost. We decided to come back the next day.

On Sunday, May 13th, we went to the 5 p.m. Evensong Service. We arrived early. Everyone was in silent meditation at the Abbey. A few minutes later the organ began playing softly in the background and then a grand crescendo as the choir arrived

"This is a place for prayer and meditation," said the program. I was touched by the beautiful music and the silence. Three men in their 70s, wearing red robes with blue collars sat in the 3 chairs next to the choirmaster. They slept soundly through the sermon then awakened enough to take up the offering. A lady minister delivered the message. Afterwards we roamed throughout the building, stopping at length at the Poet's Corner, and looking at famous statues.

After leaving Westminster Abbey we ate at The Fuller's Ale & Pie House in the Sanctuary House Hotel. It was my first time to eat Shepherd's Pie. It was delightful.

Dates and location are important to remind us. Locations, whether in British Columbia, New Mexico, or Jerusalem, have an heir of importance in our lives. Each location has a feel, a sense of urgency, a component of energy that sways our lives. In Los Angeles Grauman's Chinese Theatre and the famous footprints of movie stars defines the city, or the Empire State Building in New York City, or the arch in St. Louis. In a spiritual journal the location defines a refined spirituality about it. In Athens, Greece, as one stands by the Parthenon, one can hear the voice of the Apostle

Paul talking about the Unknown God. Always take note of where you are. What are the locations of spirituality in your life?

The Emotional Experience

In my teaching and counseling experiences I often ask the question, "What is the shape of your life?" Answers vary but for all of us it is worth checking on the shape of our life. Are we grieving over the loss of a job, or a broken relationship, or maybe things are going great. From time to time in my journal I write one paragraph about the shape of my life. Remember, it only has meaning to us. It is a way of defining the emotional state of our life.

For instance one of the most memorable emotional experiences in my life involved a fire in which 16 people were killed. It was a nursing home across the street from our hospital. A few months after the fire, the building was torn down. I wrote a journal entry as a reminder of the event and titled it, "Building Torn Down."

The date was May 22, 2006 when the building was torn down. I wrote in my journal:

I was there most of the night, going from the critical care area and to be with families who had family members either dying or in critical condition. As the morning slowed, I went from room to room in the hospital and said a prayer for the elderly patients who had smoke inhalation, or others who were frightened. It was an emotional time as I tried to reassure the patients, many who wanted to know how their roommates were. I remember that my first cup of coffee was at 4 a.m. and I walked over to the steps of the burnt building. A lady was crying on the steps. I sat down beside her and she said, "Mom died here and it was her birthday." I can not remember a more emotional moment in my life. Tearing down the building was a reminder I tried to capture with a prayer poem in my journal.

Dear Heavenly Father,

This is a time of remembrance for us. We remember that 16 people lost their lives here.

We also remember those who performed incredible feats of sacrifice: fireman risking their lives, health care workers, patients, nursing home workers, and others who rushed through smoky corridors searching for voices hidden in the darkness.

In fear and silence the brave fought for safety for the frightened ones and brought them to a place for healing.

There are many untold stories of that night, of relatives searching for their loved ones, of doctors, nurses, and other hospital workers making room for a sudden rush of scared and injured patients and providing needed emergency care.

Today, we pray for this to be a time of healing covered with hope and new beginnings and possibilities.

May this be a place where hope replaces fear, healing replaces sorrow, and dedication brings a renewal of your healing spirit.

Amen

The emotional element we encounter each day is an important word to place in a journal. The date, the location, and the emotional experiences, are the Mind the Gap moments that can easily be forgotten. Instead, these are the frameworks of a spiritual journal, moments sanctified by God's spirit and presence in our lives.

5

A Passion for Place

An old wobbly chair under a fragile shade tree will do!

For several summers I spent several weeks divided between retreat centers in Glorieta, New Mexico, Green Lake, Wisconsin, and Ridgecrest, North Carolina. I looked at these opportunities as a place where I could not only teach others, but it allowed time for spiritual direction and searching in my own life.

I would get up early, go to the prayer garden, write in my journal and pray. It was a significant time in my life. I remember once being discouraged by our house not selling in Birmingham, Alabama, and that meant a decision had to be made about what we should do next. I remember sitting by the stream in the prayer garden at Ridgecrest Retreat Center. I prayed with little faith about the future. I remember picking up a rock and placing it in my pocket. When I went to breakfast I had a message, "The house had sold." An unforgettable memory and I still have the rock and the memories from that day.

The Power of Place

Entries in our journals represent defining moments in our lives. I grew up in a small town in East Tennessee, and to this day I am still in contact with those whom I played with, and I can still remember the way the streets looked, the RCA six-tube radio and Bible I got for Christmas when I was eleven, the rocks we threw in the Clinch River behind our house, the basketballs that rolled down the hill toward the river, and climbing through briars to catch the balls before they ended up in the river.

Clinton defines my early days. It is a PLACE ! A basketball

goal, four boys living next door, a corkball, trips to the Little League Park, band practice, and days that lasted forever.

An entry from August 26, 2006, helps define a moment in my life related to Clinton:

"I sit outside for a few moments, read Psalms, and watch Cuddles and Aidan play. A slight breeze passes periodically. In a few moments we leave for Clinton, Tennessee, for the opening of the civil rights museum—a 50 year reminder of how some things have changed."

Clinton, Tennessee, was the first high school in the nation to integrate in 1956. Time magazine wrote this story about Clinton. on December 17, 1956. I was in the 8th grade. Two years later, Clinton High School, would be blown up on my birthday, October 5, 1958.

THE SOUTH: The True Face of Clinton

Municipal election day came clear and warm last week to Clinton, Tenn. Main Street was gay with holly and Christmas lights. The Rev. Paul Turner, 33, pastor of the First Baptist Church, the community's largest, dressed slowly before setting out on a mission of importance and, as it developed, of danger. On the outskirts of town, a small band of white men glared up at the cluster of homes atop Foley's Hill, where live the Negroes whose children would try soon again to attend Clinton high school. Thus did Clinton (pop. about 3,700 law-abiding citizens and about 300 defiant segregationists), a town with a split personality, begin a critical day in its history.

Tucked away in the Cumberland foothills of East Tennessee, Clinton* is an improbable place for racial crisis. Its sons fought for the North in the Civil War (Clinton has voted Republican virtually ever since). About 800 Clintonians work for Union Carbide Nuclear Co. at nearby Oak Ridge, where, as at other federal enclaves, the schools have been successfully integrated. Most of Clinton's 48 Negro families own their own homes and have long been accepted as solid, sober members of a solid, sober (and Baptist-dry) community.

When the order to integrate Clinton high school came last January, hardly any of the townfolk liked the idea—but nearly all of them accepted it as law. Then upon Clinton descended Demagogue Frederick John Kasper, 27, a Washington, D.C. bookseller (now free on $10,000 bond while a contempt-of-court conviction is being appealed), to breathe racial fire into the quiet town. The vast majority of Clintonians remained willing to obey the law. But some followed Kasper, set themselves up as an obscene, stone-throwing vigilante group, drove the Negro children from Clinton high school (TIME, Sept. 10 et seq.).

"That'll Teach Yuh."

The town election last week offered a test of the segregationists' strength; they backed candidates for mayor and three aldermanic posts against men who were willing to accept integration. The Rev. Paul Turner offered another test; he announced that on election day he would escort Negro children from their homes to Clinton high school. Even as Clinton's voters were moving to the polls, Paul Turner walked slowly up Foley's Hill, where he was met half way by six Negro boys and girls.

Turner led the nervously smiling children through a gauntlet of racial epitaphs to the school, left them there, headed back through town. Suddenly his way was blocked by three husky men. One grabbed him. He twisted, ran headlong into another, broke away, dodged across the street and was caught again, just a few yards from one of Clinton's two polling places. Under a storm of fists, Turner fell back against a car that was soon smeared with his blood. Then he went all the way down. Others, including two hysterical women, joined the kicking, clawing, screaming mob. A man and a woman from a nearby insurance office tried to help Turner. The man was driven back and pelted with eggs; the woman was pushed against a storefront by another woman. Arriving belatedly, police broke up the brawl. Sneered one of Turner's assailants while being led away: "That'll teach yuh, Reverend."

At that point, the segregationists clearly were carrying Clinton's critical day. But they had won only a skirmish. And within minutes of the attack on the Rev. Paul Turner, a remarkable thing happened: the good people of Clinton, Tennessee, began trooping to the polls in record numbers. Recording their disgust, they swamped all segregationist-backed candidates by margins of nearly three to one, elected as mayor coolheaded, fair-minded Judge T. Lawrence Seeber, 58. This, far more than the ugly face of the mob, was the true Clinton. In it lay hope for the South.

A Conversation

In my journal from August 28, 2006, I wrote:

Alfred Williams, one of the original 12 students that walked to school with Reverent Paul Turner, sat in front of me at First Baptist Church where Paul Turner had been the pastor. Afterwards I asked him a question. "What did Rev. Paul Turner, walking with you to school mean?" (Remember that Rev. Paul Turner was badly beaten after walking with the students. People were yelling, "kill him, kill him!")

Alfred said with a great deal of pride in his eyes and voice, "Nothing meant more to us than that he stood by us during that time. He was a great man!" (Note: It was evident all weekend that Rev. Paul Turner was a hero to the African-American community. His quotes were engraved in marble on the wall outside the museum.)

When he shared his thoughts, memories of the Reverend Paul Turner brought tears to my eyes... Rev. Paul Turner, besides living next door to us in Clinton, had a tremendous influence on my life. He preached my ordination sermon at Walnut Street Baptist Church

in Louisville, Kentucky, when I was a student there in 1970. He was
always kind and gentle, always interested in what I was doing, and
a person I highly respected.

Many times, when I was in seminary, I talked to Paul Turner of the Clinton experience. In none of these conversations did he realize the importance of what he had done. He received thousands of letters, many filled with hatred, others with admiration. One was from Billy Graham, another from Edward R. Murrow. To Rev. Turner, the hatred he received was paramount. It affected the rest of his life. But I realized when talking to Alfred that "Paul Turner had done a great deed for people who were disenfranchised, worn down by hatred, beaten by public opinion, and who feared for their lives every moment." I wished he could have been there this weekend to realize the effect he had really had on people's lives.

Another Time, Another Place

The character of any day can be life changing. Sure, some days more than others, but possibility always arranges itself. On October 20, 2009, we were in Tiberus, a city that sits on the western coast of the Sea of Galilee in Israel. We had been traveling and sightseeing all day. After the big buffet supper, I went to my room and wrote in my journal:

We are tired from the travel today. The boat trip across it was inspi-
rational. Everyone was in a festive mood. The sea is tranquil and
beautiful, adding to the religious flavor of crossing the Sea of
Galilee. A playing of the United States National Anthem greeted us
on the boat. The reading of the scripture passage, from Mark 1:16,
gave us the flavor of where we were. "As Jesus walked beside the Sea
of Galilee, he saw Simon and his brother Andrew casting a net into
the lake, for they were fisherman. Come follow me," he said. We
sensed God's presence.

The trip to Caesara Phillipi was confusing, mainly because of motion sickness on the curvy mountain roads. I can see how Jesus could have been there when he talked about Peter being a rock, and also how the transfiguration could have happened there.

Capernaum was neat, and I was surprised how much of Jesus ministry was within 2 miles of that one place; the feeding of 5000, numerous healings, and the beautitudes.

I often close out the day with some thoughts from the experience. These were my thoughts that day:

Viewing a previously unseen area of the world opens new vistas of understanding.
ALWAYS remember the good from a bad situation.
Most people have no idea of the real influence of their lives on others.
Simple things often have great meaning.
There are always flowers blooming somewhere.
And finally, the big events that change our lives are often unexpected.

Saint Anne's – Another Place, Another Time

There is an old tool shed I often go to when I travel to Kentucky. It is over 60 years old. It was once painted white but is now caked in dust and falling apart. On the side is a minature made cross that has penciled beside it St. Anne's. It is nothing to brag about. It is in a place where no one would find it unless someone who knew about it led you there. It is just an out of the way place, burdened by broken limbs, dust covered, and inside filled with spider webs and an assortment of bugs. It is not a way memorable in any way, just a tool shed in the wilderness on an unused dirt road. It is certainly not on the list of most visited prayer places, or a place noted where maybe someone stopped and said the prayers for the day.

On September 3, 1952, the catholic Monk Thomas Merton wrote in his journal:

"I am now almost completely convinced that I am only really a monk when I am alone in the old tool shed Reverend Father gave me. (It is back in the woods beyond the horse pasture where Brother Aelred hauled it with the traxcavator the day before Trinity Sunday). True, I have the will of a monk in the community. But I have the prayer of a monk in the silence of the woods and the tool shed. To begin with: the place is simple and really poor with the bare poverty I need worse than any other medicine and that I never seem to get. And silent. And inactivity-materially. Therefore the Spirit is busy here. What is easier than to discuss mutually with You, O God, the three crows that flew by in the sun with light flashing on their rubber wings? Or the sunlight coming quietly through the cracks in the boards? Or the crickets in the grass? You are santified in them when, beyond the blue hills, my mind is lost in Your intentions for us all who live with hope under the servitude of corruption!

Out here in the woods I can think of nothing except God. High up in the late summer sky I watch the silent flight of a vulture and the day goes by in prayer.

You have called me into this silence to be grateful for what silence I have and to use it by desiring more. The Spirit is alone here with the silence of the world. St. Anne's is like a rampart between two existences. On one side I know the community to which I must return. On the other side is the great wilderness of silence in which, perhaps, I might never speak again to anyone but God as long as I live.

It seems to me that St. Anne's is what I have been waiting for and looking for all my life and now I have stumbled into it quite by accident. Now, for the first time, I am aware of what happens to a man who has really found the his place in the scheme of things."

When at Saint Anne's I walk softly, remember the prayers said by a small monk who thought this was heaven, and sigh with thankfulness that I too have found this place.

The Place Where You Are

Make the place where you are come alive. Dust off the squirrels that pass by, listen to the symphony of the early risers at your bird-feeler, dance with the wind, cuddle the coffee in your mouth, be awake to the storms coming, walk and listen, stitch your life together, pray for friends in trouble, write down the color of the sky, the neighbors names walking up the street, watch the deer in your back yard and tell about them, and as you write it down, BE THANKFUL! This is your day. This is your place.

6

Praying

You are here to kneel
Where prayer has been valid. And prayer is more
Than an order of words, the conscious occupation
of the praying mind, or the sound of the voice praying.
('Little Gidding,' Stanza I, T.S. Eliot)

Psalms

Prayer plays a significant part in a spiritual journal. It is like a match that sparks the spiritual flame, the home run that wins the game, the power that brings down the spirit of God. Without prayers in a journal there is a blank spiritual spot. It is almost incredulous to say, but prayless journals are not spiritual. There is something about the prayers we leave that tell us of the journey, that reflect those moments we have shared with God and want to continue to remember. The Psalms have yielded a treasure in my life. They have become my favorite book, far surpassing other scriptures.

Several years ago, Ray Waddle, former religion editor for The Tennessean in Nashville, Tennessee, wrote a book titled A Turbulent Peace – The Psalms For Our Time. It was his reflections on the Psalms. Each Psalm had a title, a key verse, some reflections, and a prayer. Following his example I began my journey praying the psalms. My initial goal was to give a title to each Psalm and a note a key verse that stood out in the passage leading me to the title.

I began by copying the Psalm and placing it in my journal, often leaving an extra blank page beside it for notes. I would carry this as a prayer, sometimes for weeks. For Psalms 1 I titled it, "A Blessed Man" and the key verse was verse 1, "Blessed is the an who does not walk in the counsel of the wicked or stand in the way of sinners or sit in the seat of mockers." (Psalm 1:1. NIV). I also read commentaries and noted that Psalm 1 was written for Solomon to his son to tell him how to live. What began as a simple journey lengthened into over 4 years to complete the project. My titles were different from Waddles but it has become one of the most important aspects of my journals, the Psalm, the blank page, the title, the meanings, and the favorite verses. This exercise has made the Psalms into a continuous prayer book that expresses every emotion that touches my life.

An Influence on My Prayer Journal

At times during our lives, a historical character leaps from the pages of a book and something happens inside of us. We see their influence, we feel the heartbeat of their life, and we become inspired to try to incorporate parts of their lives in ours.

A person of great influence to me was Saint Wulfstan of Worchester. Wulfstan was born about 1008 in the English county of Warwickshire. His family lost their lands around the time King Cnut or Canute of England came to the throne. He was probably named after his uncle, Wulfstan II, Archbishop of York. Through his uncle's influence, he studied at monasteries in Evesham and Peterborough, before becoming a clerk at Worcester. During this time, his superiors, noting his reputation for dedication and chastity, urged him to join the priesthood. Wulfstan was ordained in 1038, and soon joined a Benedictine monastery at Worcester.

After the Norman conquest of England, Wulfstan was the only English-born bishop to retain his diocese for any significant time after the conquest (all others had been replaced or succeeded by Normans by 1075). It was noted that pastoral care of his diocese was Wulfstan's principal interest. It was said that his prayers sometimes produced healings and one of the miracles attributed to Wulfstan was the curing of King Harold's daughter. In describing Wulfstan it was said, "He was humble and ready to serve wherever he was called. He gradually acquired a reputation as a holy man who could on occasion work miracles, especially on behalf of the sick. He longed for God, there was always a psalm in his mouth and Christ ever in his heart."

The Prayer Book
I had also read somewhere that he carried a prayer book with him that contained prayers that he had copied or written himself. It was that unfound prayer book that influenced me. Supposedly there are copies but I have never seen one.

The best I can discover is that he took one of the regular prayer books of that day and included his own private prayers. As I thought of those words, "there was always a psalm in his mouth and Christ ever in his heart," I began adding prayers to my spiritual journal. The real purpose was so that as I went about my daily ministry as a hospital chaplain I could use prayers in both a healing context, or as inspiration for God's guidance my own life.

The effect of the prayers on my life became significant. I came to a conclusion that the prayers we say each day are the most important thing we do. Examples of some of the prayers in my journal include one of Dietrich Bonhoeffer, written in prison before his execution.

O God, early in the morning I cry to you.
Help me to pray
And to concentrate my thoughts on you:
I cannot do this alone.
In me there is darkness,
But with you there is light;
I am lonely, but you do not leave me:
I am feeble in heart, but with you there is help;

I am restless, but with you there is peace.
In me there is bitterness, but with you there is patience;
I do not understand your ways,
But you know the way for me....
Restore me to liberty,
And enable me so to live now
That I may answer before you and before me.
Lord, whatever this day may bring
Your name be praised.
Amen

Another prayer that stands at attention when I read in the prayer section of the journal is one written by Brother Paul Quenon, a monk at the Abbey of Gethsemani, in his book "My Silence is the Lord."

Turn into My place, and sit quietly.
Drink from My stream and My vintage.
Cast off your shoes, discard your hardships
And listen to My evening song.

I seek a heart that is simple.
With the peaceful I spread My tent.
I will wash your feet and dry them.
My silence will be their perfume.

And of course the Bible prayers are found throughout the scriptures. One of my favorites is, "Let us then approach the throne of grace with confidence, so that we may receive mercy and find grace to help us in our time of need." (Hebrews 4:16)

My friend, Robert Benson, has written a book called Living Prayer, which I consider one of the best books on prayer I have read. These are the words from that book that I wrote in my spiritual journal.

"When you pray begin by praising God for the gifts and graces that you have been given. Then confess who you are in relation to God – the good and the bad, what binds you closer to God and what separates you from God, what you can do and what you cannot do, what you love and what you fear. When you are empty enough, you may indeed begin to hear God's Word for you." (p.25)

Every time I read that passage, emotion fills me. It is a continuous reminder to me of the importance of getting empty enough to begin to hear God's Word. This is the power of a spiritual journal. Words are not handed down easily. The words in it are Godlike messages that apply to me! As I carry these words in my journal, I am never far from the holy moments of God's voice. In this case, the prayer was added on March 12, 2000, a Sunday in Gadsden, Alabama. I do not know if it was raining, sunny, or cloudy, but I do know that God spoke to me.

As I practiced the prayers that attracted my attention I found myself writing my own prayers and placing them in my journal. Reading others prayers became an inspiration that freed my own hand to try to record my words to the Father.

This was a prayer which I used at a funeral service for a lady who had committed suicide and left thousands of persons with many questions in their own lives.

For Lucy
In our sorrow today
God give comfort for our fragile spirits.
We are like a toy broken
Afraid
Dreading the darkness.
But Father be our courage
So that we might see light
Even in the Darkness.

Have mercy upon us
Touch our lives with your love
Be our strength and our shield

Give us patience
Patience with our brothers and sisters
Let us not judge others falsely
But seek to give comfort and hope
To all who are weak.

May Your protection surround us
For we trust in Your unfailing love.

As our spirit grows faint with us
It is You who know our way.

Holy Father
Give us grace to sustain us
A sympathetic heart that hears
The cries of those in despair
And give us healing mercies
So that everyone we touch
May be recipients of your Love.

Through Jesus Christ Our Lord.

Amen

Prayers touch us. Many ours, some others, maybe even a Psalm quoted at midnight. Prayers are precious reminders. They define the moment, clothe it in His Presence, and awaken new possibilities in our lives. Prayers show how God has worked in our lives.

It's Prayer Time Again

Many times as I walk down the halls of the hospital where I am chaplain I see the needs on people's faces. Perhaps it is a meager smile, a half-hearted hello, a frowned brow, the heaviness in the walk, and no time for humor. The times can be tough and I can tell by the requests on the prayer list. "Brother Dan, please add me to your prayer list!

The prayer list grows heavy and sometimes I wonder, "What does this praying really mean?" When overwhelmed, we need the prayers of others to sustain us. I still remember the Apostle Paul's words to the church at Corinth, "You help us by your prayers." (2 Corinthians 1:11)

Those words encourage me, encourage me to realize that prayers do make a difference! In my journal are the prayer pages, I turn my journal over and write from the back pages like I do the front, but that is where the prayer requests are listed. It is usually broken down in sections with a lengthy list of names: those with long-term illnesses, many who have passed on. There is a journey's list; those who are searching for employment, family relationships broken, some faced with indecision, a missionary in China, a church in Montana, and these are followed by the surgeries, persons undergoing surgery this week. A section for our family is placed by itself to remember the dying aunt, an uncle who has fallen and has broken bones, a cousin who just found out he has prostate cancer. It can be a lengthy list. A final section is the thanksgiving section; the new grandson, a surprising gift of a Pelikan fountain pen, someone asking me to do a spirituality retreat, the person – a longtime friend- who fixed my lawnmower, the newlyweds whom God had brought together, a house that has sold, a miraculous healing, a nice vacation in Cancun, maybe even thanks for a smile at the right time that encouraged me.

Snippets

In a sense these prayer requests are like snippets in our lives. They are short, refined moments, searching for a place to layer themselves. A journal is a good place for them, maybe not perfect, but just the writing down of a name, or an event, or a thanksgiving, can be a sacred moment. They are reminders of the moments when God, hiding in the shadows, blesses us and we are not aware until it is over.

My journal sometimes is filled more with scratchy notes because the timing was short and there was not time for more words. These notes become hints at the Divine refreshment, moments when I knew the availability of God. The following began as short notes and then were refined into the happenings of those days. These praying days are a reminder of moments when I knew that God had answered a prayer and I wept with thanksgiving.

Snowing in Michigan

The date was December 23, 2004. I was in my brother-in-law's house in Canton, Michigan. It had snowed all night. Eight inches of snow surrounded the house. It was a typical cold Michigan night with flakes generally circling in the air. I was getting ready to go to Chelsea Community Hospital to take my wife, Janet, back to Tennessee. This was her third week in the hospital and it had been a difficult time for her.

Late the night before we had received a call that Janet's dad, 88 years old, had fallen and was in terrific pain and couldn't move. They were having difficulty getting medical help for him. His wife, Georgia, my mother-in-law, was trying to help and she had earlier in the year had major open heart surgery. We were worried. What to do? But 649 miles away there is not much you can do but pray.

Then, that same morning, on December 23rd, I received a phone call from my daughter Melinda. "Dad, Aunt Suzanne called and she was hysterical." My daughter told me that Eric

(Janet's other brother) had been in a terrible wreck on the interstate 65 in Nashville. It had been snowing all night and ice had covered the roads in Tennessee. It was a major ice storm. And someone at the wreck scene had used Eric's phone to call his wife and told her she had better come quickly to where the wreck was because he was in such bad shape.

Do you get the picture? Wife Janet in hospital and I am going to get her out of the hospital to take her back to Tennessee, even though she did not feel well. Her father in need of immediate medical help, and her brother may be dead in a car wreck.

Surrender to God in prayer is not easy. Our dependence becomes totally on Him during such a moment. It is a time when he has the opportunity to show his mercy and love.

Those were the longest minutes of my life. Minutes were shaped into partial hours. Every moment a dread. It 650 miles away, my sister-in-law, Jan and I could only pray.

I could just feel the terrible numbing of saying to Janet in the hospital, good news, your dad is alive. Bad news! Eric is dead!

I immediately began calling hospitals: Centennial, Vanderbilt, Baptist, Southern Hills !! Do you have an ambulance that has gone to get Eric Honeycutt who was involved in a wreck? NO ! NO! NO! NO!

The worse fear. Eric Dead!! That would be the worse tragedy that could hit our family for many reasons. Then Melinda called again saying that Eric's eight year old son called and said he was in Centennial Medical Center where I worked.

I called the ER again! Kim answered. "Brother Dan, I believe he is here. He's with Lee. Let me get you into that room."

The next voice I hear is Lee Trevor and in the distant background Eric with groping words saying something almost understandable. "Lee, is he alive?" "Brother Dan, well yes. He is bruised really badly and probably has a concussion, but I believe he is going to be ok."

Do you have any idea how comforting my friend Lee's voice

was in a life and death situation 650 miles away? Just the news, "he is going to be ok!" My sister-in-law and I both began weeping and just said THANK YOU LORD FOR ANSWERING PRAYER!!!

Praying Time Again

So it's that time again. The journal is open to the prayer section. "You help us by your prayers," says Paul, and I remember someone once saying, "the greatest thing you can ever do is be the answer to someone's prayer."

It is time to go over the list once more. Kim is number 1, her days numbered. Ed needs a job. Some of us need renewed direction. Our leaders have a tough job. Pray for guidance for them that God may give them the right directions. Pray for the person in the office next to you. Pray that they may have a good day, a day of good news and hope and that their family may be well.

Pray for yourself, that God will surround you and protect you and make his presence so clear that you can honestly say, "Thanks you Lord for answering my prayer." It's praying time again.

7

The Unexpected Guest

"Be not forgetful to entertain strangers: for thereby some have entertained angels unawares." (Hebrews 13:2, KJV)

In my journal are pages set aside for special notations. In the front of my spiritual journals is a page dedicated to listing people who have changed my life. They are the unexpected guests! Each name reflects a time when the person named did something that changed the direction I was going. It could be a person who offered me a job, someone who shared their life at an important time with me when I was struggling, or the person who sent a Christmas gift during a period of unemployment. These unexpected guests have some commonalities. They were all, I believe, sent by God. They came as angels unaware. They were life-changers, sent at the appropriate time with special gifts that I needed.

The Tap on the Shoulder

It was one of those requests for a 6 a.m. visit before surgery. Some of these can be strange, like the man who didn't want prayer, but just a witness as he changed his will and wrote it on the back of a napkin.

This request was also unusual. The request was for me to walk with the patient from his room to surgery. This was a first for me. Usually, I prayed for a patient and left the technicians in charge. After our short conversation and prayer, the attendant began moving the bed toward the door. When it was almost to the door I reached out to Maria, the patient Rick's wife, and said, "Here is a prayer by Thomas Merton I often pass out to patients.

She glanced at the prayer, then her husband Rick began to cry. Maria said, "Last night before he went to sleep he said: I wish I had that prayer by Thomas Merton." Tears came to my eyes then. I knew something special was going on.

The Prayer by Thomas Merton
My Lord God,
I have no idea where I am going.
I do not see the road ahead of me.
I cannot know for certain where it will end.
Nor do I really know myself, and the fact
that I think that I am following your will
does not mean that I am actually doing so.
But I believe that the desire to please you
does in fact please you. And I hope I have
that desire in all that I am doing.
I hope that I will never do anything apart
from that desire. And I know that if I do
this you will lead me by the right road
though I may seem to be lost and in the
shadow of death. I will not fear, for you
will never leave me to face my perils alone.

From Thoughts in Solitude
Rick held the prayer in his hand during the surgery. The report afterward was dismal. This young man and his wife, both recent graduates of Sewanee Divinity School, with an 8 year old daughter, Chloe, and 5 year old son, Maxx, who were soon to be fatherless.

I can't tell the blessings I received during those last weeks of Rick's life. He was here for 5 weeks. Daily there were the prayers, the Merton chats, and the moments of silence when the pain was deafening. There were times I couldn't pray very well because my own tears got in the way.

Rick improved enough to go back to Sewanee for a couple of weeks. I participated in his **ordination** service, surrounded by his many friends from Sewanee, many of them in long white robes and me in my best suit.

It was one of the most memorable religious services in my life. God's presence was there.

It was a hopeful time, possibly he might live for a couple of years. They would soon be moving to North Carolina where Maria would be an associate priest at a parish. Rick was already planning a book about his experience.

Two weeks later Rick was back in the hospital. The doctor sat on the bed and in hushed tones said, "2 to 3 weeks is all that is left." For hours after that I would glance through the window and see Maria and Rick hand in hand talking.

A day or so later they moved him to the Alive Hospice Residence. Time was slowing running out, but each day there were prayers and friends and family.

On a Thursday night his friends from Sewanee came to have a final eucharist: his pastor, the campus minister, his children, and his in-laws. His son Maxx sat on the bed beside his Dad. Everyone said what they were thankful for in Rick's life and each shared something meaningful. Maxx said he would miss his Dad. Rick closed the time by sharing Merton's prayer.

Reverend Susanna Metz went back to Sewanee and preached a sermon about Rick and the Merton prayer. She compared Merton and Solomon and Rick. She says in her sermon:

"God is pleased that Solomon, as he faces a new phase of his life, acknowledges his dependence on God and trusts God. Merton puts it: "I know that if I do this you will lead me by the right road though I may know nothing about it. Therefore will I trust you always though I may seem to be lost and in the shadow of death." But that's all well and good for Solomon— it's all well and good for Merton. They're two very famous men. Could we compare ourselves to either? I'm watching my student prepare for death with incredible courage and I say to myself, "Where did he get this? For heaven's sake, I was his teacher and I wonder if I'd have anywhere near his trust in God's care." I don't know, but that's where scripture and prayer and the example of others really help."

I went to see Rick several times after that. Each day he grew weaker, but still very peaceful. One day I was talking to him and he seemed to transpose earth and enter this side of heaven. He said, "Someone is tapping me on the shoulder." Another time he said, "I never realized all the possibilities there would be in heaven."

On Thursday night, July 28th, 2006, I was with Maria for a couple of hours. Rick could only shed a tear now and then, or move his eyebrows. I read from the Psalms and Maria lay her head on his arm.

Maria shared what a blessing the Doctors had been here, the staff, those who helped with the journey. A friend Donna had come from Michigan to be with her. Everyone else had left. About the time the friend got back I left. At 8:37 p.m. Rick passed away. He is at peace!

Afterwards

On my blog I wrote about Rick. I received comments from several of his friends. Doris Westfall wrote:

"I am a friend and fellow classmate of the Hoeckers. I too was at their ordination, my first act as a priest, ordained only 5 days before. They were the true priests there that evening. I just returned from Sewanee and Rick's memorial service. Words cannot express what this couple have given to their friends in their faithful witness to the love and compassion of Jesus Christ in sharing their difficult journey. I am privileged to call them my friends".

And his friend Kurt Schlanker wrote:

"Thank you so much for your postings and your friendship with Rick and Maria. The Hoeckers were the first friends that I made when I moved to Atchison 14 years ago. Rick, Maria and I taught together, and did plays at the local community theater together. It was the example of Rick and Maria, along with the intercession of Christ, that caused me to walk into the doors of Trinity Episcopal Church in Atchison, after many years as a hard core (some would probably say hard headed) atheist. Rick was a sponsor at my baptism 8 years ago. I am grateful that he was a part of my life and was my friend. He was supposed to be a groomsman in my wedding in June, but was too ill to attend. I carried a picture of Rick, Maria, Chloe, and Max in my tux pocket. I know they were there. A week before he passed, I got to talk to him and tell him that I loved him (I do not believe in saying goodbye, as I don't think our loved ones truly leave us). Rick told me he loved me. Rick was a dear, true friend, and my life has been enriched by knowing him."

I still keep in touch with Maria, and Chloe, and Maxx, via facebook. Chloe is a young lady, Maxx is all boy, and Maria's poems and spirituality still amaze me. As I said, keep a place in your journal for special people who pass your way. Don't miss them, they may be THE UNEXPECTED GUEST!

8

Storms

"I will give you the treasures of darkness, riches stored in secret places, so that you may know that I am the Lord." (Isaiah 45:3)

The sun is shining. It is late April. We have plans to go shopping, take our puppy Cuddles to the vet, buy some groceries, and take a nap this afternoon. As the morning quivers forward, a tiny shadow begins to emerge in the west, a darkened cloud or two. Then a breeze steps up and limbs begin to sway. A fire alarm goes off in the distance, signifying a storm is brewing. We wait it out. The minutes pass slowly. It is getting darker outside. Hail begins to fall. There is a silence, then the wind stammering along once more, pulling at our house. We hear a tree limb break and then solid rain vigorously filtering down through the clouds. The storm is passing. The lights go out.

Storms are like that. Sudden! Something we are not prepared for, and in some cases they change the direction of our lives. During such periods we live with the bits and pieces of life, strings of time limply pass, we do not feel well, and sometimes we can't even get out of bed. There is uncertainly about us. The tiny flakes of Psalms is all that we seem to be able to read. During such periods of life, Psalm 88, speaks to me. I have titled that Psalm in my journal and Bible as *"Sitting in Darkness."* "My soul is full of trouble, my life draws near the grave, I am a man without strength, my eyes are dim, the darkness is my closest friend."(Psalm 88: 3,4,9,18)

Journaling
Writing in my journal about the storms can be difficult. I often

write on the flyleaf of my journals that "a journal is a place to wrestle with angels and struggle with demons." It is not a period in our life of bragging while writing. More than likely it is like a string of unstoppable hiccups. When we relive these moments we find ourselves weighted down. We take a deep breathe, then another. Then we move forward with the next mountain to climb. And when we cry out we only hear returned the echo of silence.

Rereading some of my journals during a stormy and unstable period I find words like this; "I am frozen in time. Afraid, I am like a hopeless drunk looking for the next fix. I feel like Samuel, "Samuel was troubled, and he cried out to the Lord all that night." (1 Samuel 15:11)

My theme seems to be Psalm 143:3-4. "The enemy pursues me, he crushes me to the ground; he makes me dwell in darkness like those long dead. So my spirit grows faint within me; my heart within is dismayed."

You know the feelings, right? There is a stormy divorce or you delicately step around your job to keep from getting fired or of offending the boss. Life becomes a stalemate. Every moment seems fragile. You are afraid to talk for fear of saying the wrong thing. The cards have changed. We are playing with an empty heart, part of us desperately gone. Aliveness has exited our lives. Our emotions get the best of us. We grow tearful, eat fractions of a sandwich, and seem to have no control over anything that happens. Our bad emotions win. Someone described it this way, "There is a knot in the heart."

To Be Honest

To be honest, re-reading the stormy parts of a journal may not be fun but they greet us with flashbacks that show God at work in us. They remind me of my failures, of dreams that failed, of persons who were once part of my life, of the grief of too many deaths. The words are like a moment captured that needs to be free us and let us alone. It rarely does. There is so much emotion, so many that we loved and remember. It is like King David running from Absalom, "why, why, why?" It is like Bathsheba waiting for Uriah. It is like Stephen standing before the fatal rock throwers that would take his life.

Ok, that is enough. What lessons can we learn from the storm we have so fragilely placed in our journals.

Lessons From the Storms

There are some lessons to learn while we are in the storm. **Storms happen suddenly** and often are without warning. You really can't plan for them. In spite of watching local television, the tree still fell down, and the patio furniture is in various states of disarray. Many of our hospital patients are like that. Suddenly, without warning, their health is in critical condition. There is a massive heart attack. Family members are called. Everyone is in shock and it falls to us to try to help them during this period in their lives.

Storms also do damage that needs repairing. It takes time, sometimes long periods of time, to repair the damage. Not only does the electricity need to be fixed for 60,000 of us, but healing requires time, skill, a softening spirit to hear the urgent cries, a compassionate heart, and someone to listen. That is part of each of our roles, to provide a compassionate spirit that provides a healing for the spirit of illnesses.

Storms often require the help of others. It takes patience and the help of others to clean up after a storm. We can not do it alone. I remember a recent tornado 20 miles away. As a church we spent a day cleaning up the limbs and trees that were broken. We are all on the front lines when the storms come. We can even be angels of mercy, bringing hope when all has been broken. We might even be the "answer to someone's prayer."

Finally, storms are not easily forgotten. They become pivotal moments in our lives. Things we remember in spite of everything else. And if we are lucky, they make us stronger, more sensitive to the needs of others, and more helpful to others when they go through the storms.

Treasures in the Darkness

In my journal I often write of the storms, the times when my emotions do not reflect my belief, times when things were out of control. The question then becomes, *"what are you doing with the storms in your life?"*

For me there is an ancient answer from the Apostle Paul. He gives reasons for suffering and for the storms when he says, "God of all comfort who comforts us in all our troubles, so that we can comfort those in any trouble with the comfort we ourselves have received from God."(2 Corinthians 1:3-4)

I had prostate cancer a few years ago. It was a shock. What if my time was almost up? How do I prepare for this journey? How quickly can we do the surgery? Thankfully, the operation was a success, but since then, when someone else gets a diagnosis of prostate cancer, I can share my own experience, even down to the best diapers to use after the surgery. You see, my experience was not for me only. It was a way for me to be an apostle of mercy to those undergoing the same thing.

Pete Wilson, pastor of Crosspoint Community Church, in Nashville, Tennessee, once preached a sermon in which he said, "The Messes of our life become the Message of our lives." The same is true of the storms. "The storms we have been through become the way of us helping others who are going through the same thing." That to me is important. What we go through, the trying moments of darkness, become the message for our lives. We should be thankful to God for that. In my journals I have plotted the stormy periods of my life. I often go back and review the choices I made. And it is fascinating to me that I would not be where I am had I not gone through some significant storms.

The Bible talks of Treasures of Darkness, riches stored in secret places. The discovery of a journal, stored for many years in a dusty drawer and hidden beneath unread stacks of paper, may be a hidden treasure, describing the storms, the disappointments, and the activities of God in our lives.

Re-reading my journals is like a treasure hunt. I am always coming on the unexpected like a recently re-read a spiritual journal from 1972. There were some important family items; the death of my grandfather, Homer L. Phillips, and my uncle Harold Davies. While searching through this journal, I found I found a copy of the first check I received from preaching, $15 dollars from the Beacon Light Baptist Church in St. Charles, Virginia. As I fumbled briefly through this intersection of time from the past and now, I also discovered a lost treasure beneath the journal, something I had misplaced, 37 letters my father had written to my mother while he was fighting in Germany during the latter days of World War II. I was only a little over a year old, but he mentioned my name in all of them.

These old journals, gathering dust, and often forgotten, have captured treasures of darkness. There is a landscape of suffering and notes about the struggle to be what God would have me to be. There are the treasured mountaintops, and especially noteworthy, the guidance received through the vigils of the dark hours, the treasures of darkness.

The Calming

It is October 20, 2009. We spent the night in Tiberius, Israel, and rode a boat across the Sea of Galilee. The sea was calm. The sun was shining. We sang the National Anthem, Amazing Grace, read the scriptures, and danced. It was a festive journey across to Kibbutz Ginosar where the Jesus Boat Museum was located.

The Jesus boat was found in 1986 by Moshe and Yuval Lufan. They said when they found it, "a double rainbow appeared in the sky." The boat evidently was made in the first century, during the time of Jesus ministry. It was discovered because of a lengthy drought that left it exposed.

As we traversed the sea, I could not help but be reminded of a trip Jesus disciples took. Jesus stayed behind to pray after the feeding of the five thousand. The disciples went ahead, but the "disciples were straining at the oars, because the wind was against them ... it was about the fourth watch of the night." (Mark 6:48)

The fourth watch of the night. It is the most susceptible point of danger for us all. We are worn out from the journey. We seem to be going nowhere. Like the disciples, we are worn out sailors. The journey has gone on much longer than we expected. The storm and clouds are pushing us and we are going nowhere.

Does this sound familiar? Each of us has our storms, times when the winds are against us, and we do not know which way to turn. We are fearful. We are scared. We feel the loneliness. It is then, when captured by the darkness and beyond any hope of survival, that God's presence appears, and Jesus says, "Take courage! It is I. Don't be afraid ... And the wind died down. They were completely amazed." (Mark 6:50-51) When they least expected it, there was one who could calm the waves, a treasure in the darkness.

Yes, when light is at a minimum and we must go on faith is where Jesus suddenly appears and the storm becomes a calm, and we rest and go to sleep in the boat, knowing that the one who loves us has shown us his love and brought us peace. My journals remind me of that peace!

9

Days of Recollection

"Each of you is to take up a stone on his shoulder ... to serve as a sign among you. These stones are to be a memorial to the people of Israel forever." (Joshua 4:4-7, NIV)

This day is a dedicated to God for the purpose of putting on paper the answer to the questions, "What is God drawing me to? What is causing my heart to stir within me?" And it is a time to reflect on what God is doing in my life.

One of the most important times for me in keeping of a spiritual journal is what I call a Day of Recollection. I usually plan this day in advance. This day is a day when the telephone has been turned off, a place has been selected that becomes a part of the journey. Some of the places I have used include sitting by a railroad track (especially important because my father and grandfather were railroaders) and remembering my family past, next to a Vietnam Monument where the person who taught me to swim is listed as a fatality of that war, a campground sitting alone in a portable chair, inside a lonely church, sitting by a lake at sunrise, alone on the beach listening to the waves with a book in my hand (usually A Gift From the Sea by Anne Morrow Lindberg), sitting in a busy cafeteria, by a stone wall covered in prayer, walking along a desert path, listening to a new born baby cry, or on a boat crossing the sea of Galilee.

The place is not nearly as important as the mood. On these days I carry my journal, a couple of ink pens, maybe a lunch with a sandwich and chips, and some water. It is a precious time. A time dedicated to remembering and seeking to understand what God is doing in my life.

Writing in my journal is a little different on these days. Normally, it begins with silence for at least 15 minutes, followed by readings from scripture that are adapted according to need, then prayers. This is followed by walking. I spend a lot of time walking during a day of recollection. It refreshes my spirit and helps me reflect.

The Notebook Journal

In the journal there is a continuous streak of writing. Since I try to do this once a month I often write down the important things, sort of a summary, of the month. This includes scriptures that were meaningful, events that happened (like a grandchild being born), examples of God's love, maybe even a list of things for which I am thankful. What happened this month worth remembering? Re-reading the journal entries for the month are helpful.

Another important way of recollecting is not limiting oneself to this month but to ones entire life. It could be you are reliving a trigger event in your life, some grief that is difficult, maybe a relationship that has soured, or some really neat remembrances; the boat ride around Manhattan, riding the elevator to the top of the Empire State building, walking through Westminster Abbey for the first time, seeing the Parthenon in Athens, watching a boat race down the Ohio River, listening to Mel Torme at a concert, riding one's daughter on the back of a bicycle, teaching a course to willing listeners at 7:30 in the morning. The list could go on. It is a good exercise, the memories stored within us that remind us of where we have been and may even be a guidance for where we are going.

Likewise we may wish to deal with the hindrances to our lives. Our hurts, our grief, our deceptions, may need to be reflected upon in this environment.

Preparation for a Day of Recollection

In my journal is a page I written by Evelyn Underhill about a preparation for a retreat that strengthens the importance of silence and a place during a time of recollection:

"A few hours ago, we were in the midst of our bristling lives, reacting all the time to the outside world. Now we enter the silence in which we will try to readjust our balance and attend to all that we usually leave out.

We come into retreat because our lives are busy and hurried and we feel the need of getting beneath the surface, of being for a time alone with God in that inner world where we discover His presence and reality. We have this lovely place, soaked in love and prayer, where everything we see and hear is calculated to lead us deeply into God –where nothing is meant to be done except for His service. We want to make the most of the influences.

The way we enter a retreat is important. Often, we waste the first day getting our bearings. I want to speak especially to those at their first retreat. I remember my own first retreat and the apprehension and vagueness with which I entered. But what a wonderful revelation it was! I remember my alarm at the idea of silence, the mysterious peace and light distilled from it, and my absolute distress when it ended and the clatter began.

Silence is the heart of a retreat. We get away from the distractions of talking, interchange, and action. We sink into our souls where God's voice is heard. Without silence around us, the inward stillness in which God educates and molds us is impossible. We come to rest before God, to find space for brooding and recollection in which we possess our souls and learn His will.

It is an elected silence. We cannot find it in the world. We must come together in a special place, protected by our own

rule from distractions, interests, and surface demands. We
have for our examples, Enoch who silently listened for the
voice of God in order to discern the divine will, and Teresa,
quiet and alone in her watchtower. The silence of this hour is
full of God's voice. Treasure that silence. It will do far more
for your souls than anything heard at our services. These
times together are only meant to I keep you pointing in the
right way and to help you to best use your silence.

Remember, silence is more than non-talking. It is a
complete change in the way we use our minds. We lead very
active lives. One thing swiftly succeeds another. Our mental
machinery is so made that the more active our work, the more
incessant the whirr of wheels, the harder it is to be quiet in the
divine present. Yet *nothing* so improves that active work as
such quietude, the sense of eternity, and the restful reception
of the Holy Spirit, ceasing all introspection and all altruistic
fidgets. Only in such a silence can we look out of our
workshop window and see the horizons of the spiritual world.

Our deepest contacts with God are so gentle because they
are all we can bear. We need quiet to experience them. They
do not come as an earthquake of mental upheaval or in the
scorching fire or rushing wind of emotion. In the silence,
there is nothing devastating or sensational, but only a still
small voice."

The Lifegiver's Gift

During a recent Day of Recollection I kept re-reading about an
event that had touched my life. I had written the story in my
journal and each time I read it, its meaning intensified in my life.

It began as an attempt to find places of spiritual importance
to people who were in a hospital setting and wished and prayed
for a sense of guidance during periods of crisis in their lives.
There were the expected places; the interfaith chapel, a water
fountain where little children could throw pennies, a quiet bench

in a garden area, and the coffee shop where people drank coffee, chatted and prayed.

An unexpected place was a bench in the women's hospital where there was a bronze statue of a young lady holding a small child in her arms. Many times, during the past decade, sometimes in the middle of the night, I have entered the hospital for an emergency or death of a child, I have stood by the statue for a moment before going to the emergency. It has always been a special inspiration to me.

There are no notations above the statue. No name. No title. After asking around, I found one person who knew the name of the artist, Elizabeth MacQueen. Further research on the internet indicated the artist lived in Mexico. An email was sent and the artist responded, "Yours is the first feedback I have gotten, other than friends going to see the piece, and I thank you for it." (I was surprised by that statement, knowing that daily people, and especially children, stopped to rub the head of the statue.)

Elizabeth MacQueen wrote:

"I adopted my daughter at birth, Mary Elizabeth, who is now 20 and the model for the piece. I brought her into this world and cut her umbilical cord via her lifegiver. I created this word for my daughter when she asked me, "How was I in your tummy Mama," at the age of 6. So I came up with a story called The Lifegiver's Gift. "You came on a star in the middle of the night. I think we saw you riding in that light. Into your Lifegiver's tummy you flew, all warm and cozy while you grew and grew." My daughter would not get enough of me reciting it again and again. When she met her lifegivers at 10 years of age, she said, "Hi! Where are my brothers?" I showed this term to a psychologist and she asked if she could use it with a patient of 40 years old as he is still having problems with his "Mother" giving him away. She used the term and has said I could use her name as a reference.

I told Mary Elizabeth that she only had one Mother and that was me, but you were blessed to have your Lifegivers Kim and Steve. In 2010 we have so many ways a child can be created and many of them leave bad feelings of a "Mother" giving them away, a "Mother" who was poor, "A Mother who was abusive," so I brought my daughter up with the term Lifegiver, *the one who gives you life*, which I find so much more an illuminating sacrifice of giving up their love child so that the child will have parents, a mother/father to raise them. Just being pregnant does not make one a mother, birth or otherwise ... they are the Great Lifegivers. We women are remarkable through and through."

She concluded, "Thank you again for your lovely message." Warmly, Elizabeth.

I passed the story of Elizabeth to many people I work with and dozens of people responded how the statue had touched their lives during difficult and important times.

Reflections

In my journal, on that Day of Recollection, I read the stories from the past and spent time in gratitude and thankfulness. Many times in reading the stories I am reminded of gifts from God that are found in the journal. As I continue to read, I wonder how many times we have passed a gift from God and missed it?

Once a week, I ask myself the question, "What has God done in your life this week that only He could have done?" Usually, he has spoken! My hope is that I have not missed it. To me, the Day of Recollection, is a sacred day. It is a day for remembering, writing down the blessings in my journal, and looking for the hints for a new tomorrow, a place where God Has Spoken!

10

Fragments

"Afterward the disciples picked up seven basketfuls of broken pieces (fragments) that were left over." (Mark 8:8)

What to Do With the Leftovers

In my journal are scraps of odd mixed items collected from assorted venues around the world; theatre tickets, plays I have attended, movies for a lazy Friday night, baseball game tickets scattered from Atlanta to Los Angeles, a ticket from the Broadway Play The Lion King, a cab driver's card from Jerusalem, a London bus pass, a Larry Biittner 1983 baseball card, emails that I don't want to lose, obituaries, and even quotes from those who have ventured into my journaling website.

"Dear Brother Phillips, I was really delighted to find your information about spiritual journaling. I have been journaling since I was 12 and in recent years, since I have become a parent, it has been my wish to have journals with much more depth to them. If I were to die suddenly, I would want my children to have a view into my heart. In the beginning, I used to just write down my complaints, but now I am desirous to expand my entries to include other things. I am currently reading the Imitation of Christ and I hope to include my responses to it." (KM)

In the fragment section of my journal I find a question. What inspires me? And, I answer:

A prayer
A Biography of a wise man

Cloisters
A lake, the sea, pounding waves
A dying man's last words
Saying goodbye
A film: American Saint
Water
Newspapers
A voiceless sermon
Love's silence
Saturn's rings
Jupiter's moons
A white, faceless moon
A puppy's love
Lingering sunsets
A birthday candle
A child's eyes
A puppy's bark
A kiss
A bird's first song
Silence

And a summary of describing myself that says, "I draw inspiration from natural events, simple thoughts, people who smile, the countryside, sky and sea."

Leftovers

After the feeding of the four thousand people with seven loaves and a few small fish, the Bible tells us, "Afterward the disciples picked up seven basketfuls of broken pieces (fragments) that were left over." (Mark 8:8) The leftovers! The fragments! For most of us, the fragments of our lives are what really matters.

In his essay, Firewatch, July 4, 1952, Thomas Merton describes his experience of walking through the Abbey of Gethsemani with a flashlight searching for places a fire might start that would destroy the monastery. He described the colored walls of the kitchen, the furnace room, the catacombs with naked wires that dangled from the ceilings, the choir novitiate, freshly painted, with long lists of appointments for the novice confessions.

The Firewatch is "devised by God to isolate you, and to search your soul with lamps and questions, in the heart of darkness," says Father Merton, then he shares this thought, "The things I thought were so important – because of the effort I put into them – have turned out to be of small value. And the things I never thought about, the things I was never able either to measure or to expect, were the things that mattered."

Yes, the fragments, the things we did not think about, were the things that mattered.

Table Graces

The dinner hour is the perfect time for going over the fragments of a day. There is always the backward glance, the thoughts one shares of the happenings, the funny things that happened, the sadness of the day, or the joys. Sitting around the table we share the importance of the day. These are the leftovers of which life is made.

One of my favorite prayers for the dinner hour, comes from the book '100 Graces' by Marcia and Jack Kelly. In this book is this prayer:

Table Graces
God of Pilgrims
Give us always a table to
Stop at where we can
Tell our story and
Sing our song.

Father John Giuliani
The Benedictine Grange West
Redding, Connecticut

A time to sing our song to the right person may change their lives. A word spoken at twilight, a lighted fire, maybe even a postcard sent from a distant place, can make a difference.

Recently, I read a note that Father Timothy Kelly wrote about the death of Thomas Merton. For many years Father Timothy was the Abbot of the Abbey of Gethsemani. After the death of Merton in Thailand in 1968, Father Timothy wrote about receiving the news in the refectory of the sudden unexpected death of Thomas Merton. Kelly said that "Father Alphonse (an older monk) comes up to me with a postcard in his hand trying to understand Merton's death. He said, 'You know, they said he died, but I just got this postcard sent from Thailand from Merton:'

"Hi, how are you? I hope it was not too much work with cheese and fruitcake this year, and I'm going to be with the monks in Hong Kong for Christmas." It ended by saying "Behave yourself now!"

Kelly said of Merton, here Merton is over there meeting with the Dalai Lama and he took time to send a postcard to this old monk! Kelly concludes, "I was in Rome for three years and I never sent Alphonse a postcard!" Yes, that fragment postcard, with a few simple words might be the turning point in someone's life. The leftovers, the fragments may make a difference to someone. They need not be replaced.

Barzilla

I once went to Engedi, a small city on the western slope of the Dead Sea. The mountains surrounding Engedi are covered with bush, with treacherous trails through difficult portions of the hills. At the top, one sees the rugged terrain, a deep valley, not a place easily found or reached. In the Bible it speaks of this area was where David was hiding from his son Absalom. It was a place not easily found. Food was scarce. The cliffs were unreachable. Spies were nearby looking for King David.

King David expresses his fears in Psalms 42-43."God why

have you forgotten me? Why is my soul so disturbed within me?" He longs for God's house ("My soul thirsts for God.") and remembers the times he led the procession to the Temple, but he is in agony. His son Absalom, and many of David's close friends, have rebelled against him. He is running for his life. He is made fun of and is suffering. He is criticized and hurt by people's words.

It is during this time that an 80 year old man named Barzillai finds David tired and thirsty and hungry in the desert and brings to him, "bedding and bowls and articles of pottery. They also brought wheat and barley, flour and roasted grain, beans and lentils, honey and curds, sheep, and cheese from cows' milk for David and his people to eat." (2 Samuel 17:27) When asked why he did it Barzillai said, "The people have become hungry and tired and thirsty in the desert." Barzillai saw David's need and provided encouragement and food during a crisis time. The scrubby leftovers, carried over tedious terrain were all that sustained David during this period of his life.

When David was dying, he called his son Solomon and shared his last words. "Solomon, show kindness to the sons of Barzillai of Gilead and let them be among those who eat at your table. They stood by me when I fled from your brother Absalom."

What a beautiful remembrance! They stood by me! Barzillai is a fragmentary person in the Bible who most of us have never heard of, who in a difficult time, stood by David, and David did not forget.

Remembrances

I recently bought a copy of John Gunter's book, *Death Be Not Proud*, at a book sale. It is the story of his son's fight against cancer and his death at 17. To me, it was interesting that, after his son's death, he began rummaging through the leftovers, things he left behind and saved, things he treasured from his earlier days. It raised my eyebrows. When we are gone, how can people take what is left and make sense of it? Does it tell a story about us that even we did not know.

For instance it has made me think of my Mother and what was left behind after she passed in 1999. There was a bell someone gave her that they had brought from Jerusalem as a present for her. The bell sits on my desk and I ring it at appropriate contemplative moments. There is a handmade book of poems that she had written and placed in her Bible, some old pictures made with a Brownie camera and her sitting on a bicycle that we got by saving Blue Stamps. Oh yes, the elephants. Why did she collect elephants? I remember her laugh! The Davies family could laugh better than any family I have ever known. The uncles and aunts always had a good story. Laughter was part of the picture.

She was a teacher. This week I received a facebook message from a student of hers in the third grade. You could tell that Mom had made a big difference in her life, this over five decades ago. Her biscuits and cold slaw were memorable. She came to my ordination after a car wreck in which our dog Herky was killed. How difficult was that for her? It was a trip of over 400 miles.

You get the point. What about you? What will you leave behind? What will that tell us about you?

The fragments in my journal are remembrances of the presence of God in my life; a clipping from the comic Mutt'erings says, "Meditation is an honorable piece of work," a cut out Bible passage from the 23rd Psalm, notes from speakers at conferences in New Mexico, a baseball ticket for April 8, 1974, when I was in the stadium the night Henry Aaron broke Babe Ruth's home run record, a note of encouragement from a friend, a copy of For Better or For Worse from the comics, showing a father appreciating his family on Father's Day, a clipping from a church bulletin celebrating their pastor going on a mission trip, and obituaries, and quotes. This does not limit the idea of the fragments of each of our lives.

The fragments tell the story of times in our lives when God's Presence was active. Those tickets for the bus stop in London led to St. Paul's Cathedral, the taxi cab in Jerusalem took us to the Western Wall, the obituaries tell us of those people who touched our lives in a special way.

"Don't forget the fragments, the leftovers of our lives, they need to be noted in our spiritual journals because they just may be the most important things we have ever done."

11

Magical Journeys

"The clowns were dancing and the elephants were smiling."
(The Author)

For several weeks I have been carrying a book with me titled "*On Pilgrimage*," by Jennifer Lash. I rarely carry books with me, but I treasured it so that, beside the Bible, it was the only other book I carried to Greece and southern Mexico while on vacation.

Jennifer Lash discovered she had breast cancer, and after chemo and radiation, she decided she would leave her 6 children at home in the care of her husband and she would make a three month pilgrimage through France and Spain visiting Holy Places.

The shape of her journey led from Lisieux, in France, to Sandiego de Compostela, in Spain, the place evangelized by the Apostle James and a frequent pilgrimage site even to this day. She stayed in monasteries, prayed in chapels and cathedrals, lit candles for strangers, fought the continual tiredness of the cancer as it attacked her body, and found within herself a spiritual strength she had not known before, which she shared in her daily written journal.

As her journey ended she wrote, "I would like to thank all those kind people on my Journey who gave me hospitality, advice, general enthusiasm and a measure of their own experiences."

One thing about Magical Journeys in our spiritual journals is that they chronicle changes in our lives. The ordinary becomes extraordinary, the silence becomes sacred, the journey itself becomes an awakening to the holy within.

Four years after her journey ended, she passed away. Her

sons wrote of her death that "she was buried in a simple home-made coffin, under a table cloth embroidered with a map of Ireland."

After finishing the book the first time, I looked up Jennifer Lash on the internet and was surprised to discover that two of her sons are Ralph Fiennes and Joseph Fiennes, both famous actors. Her son Ralph Fiennes was nominated for an academy award for The English Patient and he shared that his mother had been *"the greatest influence on his life.*

Our Journeys

Keeping a spiritual journal is a magical journey. It is undertaken during all periods of ones' life; during times of sorrow when we feel like breaking apart and words written can not explain the depth of loss, during periods of happiness when only the word thanks is appropriate, in the winter seasons when the snows bombard pellets of life that sometimes seem eternal. In May the roses bloom near Mother's Day and during the summer, August 7th to be exact, I remember my Father's birthday, always a sacred day of remembrance, noted in my journals as Dad's Birthday.

Rereading my journals I find, and this is the most important part of this book, that each page is a reminder, *a discovery of a point in life when God was alive,* and with the tiny words that survive we find hidden treasure and a record of God's work in our life.

What about your journey? Have we seen the ordinary become extraordinary, the silence become sacred, and discovered an awakening within? And the people you met on the journey, did they become a part of your sacred journey. If they have, maybe, just maybe, *you should write it down*!

Author Profile

Brother Dan Kenneth Phillips has over three decades of experience as a minister, chaplain, writer, editor, and counselor. As a writer, his publications have been printed in over two dozen periodicals, literary journals, Sunday School curriculum, a book anthology, and numerous articles on the internet, including his travel book, Four Corners- A Literary Excursion Across America.

He is a frequent retreat leader on issues of spiritual development, the monastic journeys of Thomas Merton, spiritual journaling, grief workshops, contemplation and spirituality, and spiritual direction. His web page, How to Develop a Spiritual Journal, is frequently used in universities and churches as an example of the importance of keeping track of God's movement in one's life.

He is a graduate of Tennessee Technological University in Cookeville, Tennessee, and the Southern Baptist Theological Seminary in Louisville, Kentucky. His blog, http://danphillips. blogspot.com is updated regularly. He can be reached via e-mail at brodanphillips@gmail.com to schedule retreats and speaking engagements.

Brother Dan lives in Franklin, Tennessee.

BOOKS

O is a symbol of the world, of oneness and unity. In different cultures it also means the "eye," symbolizing knowledge and insight. We aim to publish books that are accessible, constructive and that challenge accepted opinion, both that of academia and the "moral majority."

Our books are available in all good English language bookstores worldwide. If you don't see the book on the shelves ask the bookstore to order it for you, quoting the ISBN number and title. Alternatively you can order online (all major online retail sites carry our titles) or contact the distributor in the relevant country, listed on the copyright page.

See our website **www.o-books.net** for a full list of over 500 titles, growing by 100 a year.

And tune in to myspiritradio.com for our book review radio show, hosted by June-Elleni Laine, where you can listen to the authors discussing their books.

MySpiritRadio